Blended

Navigating the Challenges and Joys of a Stepfamily

Paul and Jeannette Savage

ISBN# 979-8-218-32176-5

For more information contact:

Paul Savage - PSavage@blendedbook.org

Jeannette Savage - JSavage@blendedbook.org

Cover and Interior Design by Janelle Evangelides

Editing by Tracey Barski

contents

Foreward

When I met Paul for the first time, he struck me as a successful and gregarious guy without a care in the world. Throughout that interaction, and in every interaction since, I've learned that his journey has been anything but carefree. It seems that his zest for life is the result of the transformative work he was willing to do on himself, his faith in God, and his beloved relationships with his wife and children.

Paul's story is characterized by empathy, enthusiasm for sharing his insights, and practical wisdom. He speaks passionately about the trials and joys of blending families, and his insights carry the weight of past struggles and the hope he found in overcoming them. As someone who did the hard work to become emotionally healthy, he emphasizes therapy, patience, and communication as key ingredients for successfully blending families.

As Paul continued to share his story with me throughout a series of interviews, it became increasingly difficult to reconcile the early versions of himself he described with the man I was getting to know. His transformation from a damaged, self-centered man to a selfless and devoted family man who seeks to improve the lives of everyone he encounters is what makes his story so powerful.

When I encountered Jeannette for the first time, it felt like I was connecting with an old friend. Her warmth and openness allowed our conversations to flow effortlessly. Her account of her journey was honest and sprinkled with moments of laughter and tears. Just beneath her calm and sweet demeanor exists a justified and endearing spunkiness. Her story is one marked by resilience and unwavering faith. Behind her kind eyes and warm smile lies a tale of childhood trauma and divorce. She has refused to let those scars define her, however. Her faith and belief in a higher purpose have guided her through a variety of tumultuous experiences and ultimately, to Paul. Like Paul, it's clear through her words and actions that her priorities are her faith and her family. She also shares Paul's passion for sharing the wisdom she's earned through her experiences with others.

> *Their stories capture the complexities and beauty of blended families and confirm that successful blending is not about erasing the past, but about honoring it while also building a new narrative together.*

Throughout this process, I also had the pleasure of interviewing each of the couple's children. All now successful and well-adjusted adults, they openly and honestly shared their individual stories. I was struck by their unique personalities and perspectives, and evolving roles in their family unit. Understandably, not one of them claimed the journey has been perfect, but all highlighted things that Paul and Jeannette did to help them adjust and blend. Their stories capture the complexities and beauty of blended families and confirm that successful blending is not about erasing the past, but about honoring it while also building a new narrative together. Despite the challenges faced along the way, they've collectively embraced the journey, wholeheartedly considering themselves integral members of a unified family.

Although I am not part of a blended family, I've gained valuable insights from every single conversation I've had with the members of this family. Issues like nurturing emotional health and familial relationships are universal, and I found their willingness to honestly share their personal experiences and insights to help others inspiring. No matter where you are on the blending journey, there is much to be learned from this family!

-Jacalyn Huston

.Despite the challenges faced along the way, they've collectively embraced the journey, wholeheartedly considering themselves integral members of a unified family.

Preface

Being a stepparent, stepsibling, step-grandparent, or step-aunt/uncle is not easy. Time, work, and patience are required for success. For the last sixteen years, Jeannette and I (Paul) have worked diligently at blending our families. I was part of a stepfamily in my first marriage for twelve years. Unfortunately, I wasn't as successful as a stepparent the first time around. That's one of the reasons I wanted to write this book. Since Jeannette and I have been together, we have encountered many people who have struggled to successfully blend their families. That's the other driving force behind our desire to share what we've learned with others. My discussions with others who have struggled with this process prompted me to spend some time researching the issue.

It is estimated that there are over 100 million people in the US with a "step" relationship. That is one in three! With divorce rates over nearly 40% for first marriages and 60% for second marriages, the step relationship trend will only continue to grow. Have we been perfect in blending our two families into one? Not at all. But we have been diligent and consistent in our efforts to blend our families in a way that allows us to function as a whole, while also allowing the unique personalities that make up that whole to thrive. We're proud of our family and passionate about sharing our imperfect journey with anyone who is on a similar journey of their own.

In this book, we will share our personal stories including what we feel we did right and what we did wrong. Each of our kids will share their perspective of what it was like growing up within our stepfamily. We will also share some practical advice for blending families based on our experiences.

So, whether you are single with children and want to get married, or you are currently part of a blended family, we know this book will give you some insight into how to navigate the joys and trials of having a stepfamily. After sixteen years as a blended family, we can look back and say, "It has been so worth it, and we cannot imagine our lives without our blended family."

Introduction

Look up the word *blend* in any dictionary and you are likely to find definitions like, "To mix smoothly and inseparably together" or "to fit or relate harmoniously." These definitions do help describe the goals of the work we've done to create our blended family. I (Jeannette) had three amazing kids: Christian, Anthony, and Danie (Danielle) from my first marriage when I met Paul. He had two incredible daughters from his first marriage himself, Ashley and Mariah. Within these pages, all seven of us will share pieces of ourselves and our story with you.

This book is organized into five parts. In part one, we each share the stories of our early lives that helped shape who we are. We also share our transformational experiences with therapy and how working on ourselves helped to prepare each of us for healthy new beginnings. Finally, we share how we met, fell in love, and ultimately brought our two families together. Part two, still narrative in nature, highlights our shifting relationships with our ex-spouses as we were blending our families.

In part three, we share our insights about what we feel we did right, and what we could have done better while blending our families. This part of the book is filled with the insights we've gained through both positive and negative experiences along the way. We hope that sharing these insights might help you experience more positives on your own journey!

You will meet our children in part four. All at various stages of young adulthood, they bring a variety of background experiences, perspectives, and beautifully unique personalities to our story.

In part five, we've reflected upon the efforts necessary to maintain and strengthen all of the relationships in our blended family with faith in God and commitment to our relationship guiding us along the way.

It is also important to note that the point of view alternates throughout the book since we felt it was important to share each of our stories from our perspectives using our own voices. A change in narrator is indicated by our names in parentheses in the chapters we narrate together.

Thank you for taking the time to read our story, and we sincerely hope you'll learn from our mistakes and successes, just as we have.

Part One

Building The Base

one

Our Stories

"Childhood trauma can lead to an adulthood spent in survival mode, afraid to plant roots, to plan for the future, to trust, and to let joy in. It's a blessing to shift from surviving to thriving. It's not simple, but there is more than survival."
–Unknown

Jeannette

Our experiences are all threads that make up the intricate fabric of who we are. Though some threads may be tattered and frayed, they are all part of the fabric. My experiences growing up have had a huge impact on who I am and my ability to build the successful relationships and beautiful blended family that I have today. Some of these experiences taught me what I didn't want and helped steer many of my decisions along the way. Others helped me understand the hardships of parenting as well as the unconditional love between parents and their children.

Throughout my childhood, I knew I was loved and would have what I needed despite some of the drama and trauma that I experienced. Since my mother's parents were from a generation where love and affection weren't openly expressed, she vowed to show and tell her own children how loved we were. As I grew older, it became clear that although there were mistakes along the way, she loved us all so much and did the best she could.

My story began in Nebraska in 1966. I was part of what might be called a split family. My parents never married. My father brought the baggage of two prior marriages to his relationship with my mother. He also had five children from his previous marriages: three from one relationship and two from the other. These siblings did not live near us, so I spent little time with them growing up.

My mother was also married prior to her relationship with my dad. I have two brothers from my mother's previous relationship, and they lived with us. My oldest brother was six years older than me, so we did not have a close relationship growing up. My middle brother was always there for me, and we still have a close relationship today. Sadly, my father passed away suddenly from a brain aneurysm at the age of thirty-four. I was just two years old. As a young woman, my mother had already been through a divorce from the father of my brothers, and suddenly she was a single parent with three children. As a result of the emotional trauma my mother, siblings, and I endured when my dad died, my memories up until the age of five are a blur.

When I did share my feelings, I felt they were not validated.

As I was growing up, we didn't talk much about our feelings. I was, by nature, extremely shy and quiet. It took a lot for me to work up the courage to speak up and share my feelings. When I did, I often felt they were not validated. There was an unspoken rule that we were to not "rock the boat" and that we needed to keep up the facade that everything in our family was great and that we were happy. This was the expectation, even as my mother began making some poor choices in her relationships.

I was five when my mom met a man who would become my stepdad. I learned quickly that he was not a nice man. He had a daughter whom he didn't have a good relationship with. She had her own daughter a little younger than me who was never allowed to stay overnight when she visited. I had also heard a story about him waking up his son in the middle of the night and making him sit in the kitchen with the trash can over his head because he had forgotten to take out the trash. Hearing this story as a young child scared me. I also found out that his son had later committed suicide. Regardless of these seemingly glaring red flags, my mom stayed with him. When they married, we moved from Sidney to North Platte, Nebraska to live with him.

It was during this time that he sexually abused me. The abuse began when I was around six or seven and went on until I was nine or ten years old. As a conductor for the railroad, he would go to work every three days or so. He'd be gone for twenty-four hours because he had to take the train from North Platte to Cheyenne, Wyoming. I lived for the days he would be gone, so I could let my guard down. An enormous sense of relief washed over me when I knew for certain, that he had left. Looking back, I recall my mom seeming relieved as well. She was a more relaxed and relatable version of herself, and spending quality time with us became her priority. She would get takeout for dinner and her usual focus on housework, cooking, and catering to my stepfather's needs melted away. I still cherish memories of our evenings snuggled up on the couch watching old movies together.

When my stepdad was home, life was drastically different. We had to share our mother's time and attention once again; and her relaxed demeanor disappeared. I reverted to living in fear. I would often cower under my bed in fear of him. My mother discovered me hiding many times, but she never figured out what was going on. It was hard to understand how she couldn't see it, and I so badly wanted her to. As is common with victims of abuse, I kept it a secret.

In addition to those movie nights with my mother, there are other fond memories sprinkled throughout and between those of fear and abuse. In one, I'm five and dressed in a beautiful new dress that my mother surprised me with, seated on the floor with mom and grandma for a tea party. In others, my middle brother and I are out building forts or riding our bikes. Or we're the main characters in our various make-believe lives. When we played *house*, he was always my dog. When we played *school*, I was the teacher. Apparently, I was real bossy in those made-up worlds of ours; he still teases me about that to this day. There were also sleepovers with my grandmother which included long, carefree, bubble baths in her big white clawfoot tub. These were those safe and special moments for me that undoubtedly helped build the resilience that is so often seen in abused children.

Finally, when I was twelve, my stepfather and my mother divorced. He was having an affair with a woman with young children. I've often wondered if part of the allure was that she had younger children to abuse because my brother and I were getting older. He was obviously a very sick man. The divorce was one of the best things that had ever happened in my young life. Extreme mental and physical relief washed over me when I realized I'd never have to see him again.

About a year after the divorce, Mom met another man, a railroad worker who lived in Cheyenne, Wyoming. Her relationship with him prompted our move as a family to Cheyenne. I was a thirteen-year-old, painfully shy, insecure, victim of abuse suddenly faced with adjusting to life and school in a new place. I felt flawed, insecure, and lost. Finding my place in this new environment seemed impossible. Then I found a friend. She was a girl who may have been just as lost as I was even if in different ways. Her parents were divorced, and she split her time between their two homes. I can't say whether it was her influence, the timing of our friendship, or the combination of our personalities and background experiences, but I began making some bad choices during this time in my life.

For example, once, when my mother was out of town and had left my eldest brother in charge, my new friend and I ditched school. We took my mom's car for a spin around town. We cruised around for hours smoking cigarettes, just two insecure preteens, masquerading as rebels. Looking back at this as an adult and a parent, I think about how disastrous things could have been if we had gotten into an accident.

My time bonding with this new friend was threatened when her mom became unable to support her and her siblings. They moved to their dad's house on the other side of town. This meant she had to switch middle schools, and I was completely devastated. The move to Cheyenne had been so hard for me, and suddenly, the one person I had been able to connect with was not attending school with me anymore. My mother saw and understood what I was going through and wanted to ease my pain. Although she knew it would be a huge inconvenience for her, she let me switch schools. Every morning, she drove me all the way across town just so I could go to school with my friend.

Unfortunately, her good intentions put me on a path to even more destructive behaviors. I started drinking. On one specific day that stands out in my memory, my friend and I thought it would be fun to drink before school. Of course, I was the one that got caught. The school administrator called my mom to come in for a meeting and take me home. My mom made no attempt to hide her fury on the way home; she even threatened to spank me. When we got home, she fed me and sent me to bed. Exhausted, ashamed, and slightly relieved that being sent to bed was my punishment, I didn't dare argue. That wasn't the extent of my punishment, though. She wasted no time transferring me back to my original school. Of course, I didn't see it at the time, but it was one of the best things she could've ever done for me. She rerouted me from the path of destruction I was on and changed my future for the better.

About a year after our move to Cheyenne, my oldest brother was ready to live on his own and moved back to North Platte. My younger brother also made a move. Craving a relationship with his biological father, he went to live with him. That left just my mother and me at home, but not for long. We swiftly moved in with her new boyfriend. I remember him as a nice enough man, but even at the young age of fourteen, I sensed that he was probably not great husband or father material. We had lived with him for about two years when he let his guard down with a friend and made a sexual comment about me. That friend told my mother about it, and thankfully, she broke up with him.

After that break-up, we moved into another home of our own. Eventually, my mom started dating again, and she became attached to another man. After dating him for a few years, they got married. He had children but no relationship with them. He did try to be a dad to me, but I was a teenager who had already been through a lot, and I wasn't interested in having a stand-in dad. Experience had taught me that he could have ill intentions or be gone in an instant, so why should I bother? This time, my mother's marriage lasted about six years.

> " Looking back, I can empathize with my mother and her desire to find love, security, and support in a man. "

Looking back, I can empathize with my mother and her desire to find love, security, and support in a man. She had married young and never finished high school. She was looking for someone to support her in raising three young children. Her string of broken relationships taught me what I didn't want in a relationship. In addition to all the other tumultuous changes and feelings that come with adolescence, I was building a strong desire to grow up and have a "normal" family. I envisioned a wonderful husband and several children as part of my big, perfect, and very happy family. I couldn't wait to have that.

My mom's brother and his wife became a huge, positive influence on me during my childhood. I had the chance to go and stay with them in Colorado for a few weeks each summer and loved the stable, fun environment. I felt safe and got to be a kid. We went on family bike rides and played games, and we went to church together on Sundays. As a couple, they modeled what a good marriage looked like and their affection towards one another made it obvious that they deeply loved each other. I knew I wanted to someday have what they had. I have so much love and gratitude now for the example they were to me.

At age fifteen, I met my first real boyfriend and the man who would become my first husband. As an insecure teenage girl longing for love and security, I fell hard for him. His parents had been married for a long time, and to me, that meant that they were a happy and healthy family. I later learned that I was wrong; he also came from a dysfunctional family.

We dated for four years, mostly while he was away at college. I would go with his parents to visit him sometimes, and he would come home on weekends, holidays, and summers. Because I was dating him, I never really experienced some of the classic high school experiences like homecoming or prom, but I was content at the time. We got along well and rarely fought. Looking back, I'm grateful that I was so focused on our relationship at that time. Had he not been my priority, I could have easily veered back down a path littered with unhealthy behaviors and relationships. I was carrying a lot of unresolved trauma, but I was able put all of my energy into our relationship instead of self-medicating with drugs, alcohol, or promiscuous behavior.

My first boyfriend and I married as soon as we possibly could and moved to Denver, Colorado. He was twenty-four, and I was just nineteen years old. Looking back, I see a loyal, unhealthy, insecure, yet hopeful young girl who tended to always put others first. I see a girl that settled.

My 1st Marriage

My husband's grandfather was a pastor, so he married us. As a nineteen-year-old bride, I vividly recall getting ready to walk down the aisle and hearing the voice of God tell me, "You shouldn't be doing this." I knew in my heart that I wasn't supposed to marry the man before me, but I was and had always been a peacekeeper. I ultimately went through with it because I didn't want to hurt his feelings. Even though I ignored that voice and chose to marry him anyway, we had some good years together, and God blessed us with three amazing kids.

> Early in our marriage, I didn't really have a voice or share my opinions very often.

Early in our marriage, I didn't really have a voice or share my opinions very often. We had so little money that we could often barely afford groceries, yet he would go hunting and fly fishing, which are expensive hobbies. I'd get upset but kept my feelings to myself rather than initiating any sort of conflict. He also never picked up after himself, which drove me crazy. Rather than communicating my anger and frustration, I got into the habit of picking up after him. My learned behavior of not "rocking the boat" had carried over into my marriage.

Despite these mounting frustrations, I told myself our marriage was pretty solid. Since I am an easy-going person, and I never voiced my concerns, we rarely fought. After our first child, Christian, was born, we started going to church together. I had always known I wanted my kids to be raised within the church. When I was twenty-four, our second child, Anthony was born. By the time I reached thirty, we welcomed our third child, Danielle (Danie). I then fully devoted myself to raising my kids and being the best mother I could be. Fond memories of us as a family during this time overpower those of the marriage that was already fraying behind the scenes. We would have dinner together as a family as many nights as possible. We also did a lot of camping as a family and went on at least one vacation every summer. He coached our kids in sports, and I was always in the stands cheering them on. We definitely came together in support of our children. I felt I was well on my way to fulfilling that dream of having a big, happy family as I settled into the busy life of being a wife and mother of three young children. Life with my extended family, however, was taking a more negative turn.

It was during this time that our family secret of sexual abuse came out. After marrying, having one stepdaughter and four biological children, and going through a divorce, my brother revealed that he had been abused by our stepfather. This revelation floored me. I thought I was the only one who had experienced abuse at the hands of our stepfather. My brother shared that he was in therapy and working through the trauma and emotions stemming from the abuse.

As my brother and I connected around our shared experiences with our stepfather, he revealed that he had also been abused by our older brother. The idea that we also shared in this devastating experience was gut-wrenching for me, but the two of us did become closer because of this shared trauma. My brother's therapist recommended he confront our oldest brother and share what had happened to him with our mother. He did. As a result, our older brother who was married and living his own life, stopped talking to us and everyone in the family. Since he had become an abuser himself, we assumed that he had also suffered abuse at the hands of our stepdad. Although this is not an excuse, it did impact how I processed what he did to me and my other brother.

I have forgiven him, but unfortunately, we no longer have a relationship. When my mother learned about my stepfather abusing us, she was irate and called to confront him. He did what any abusive coward would do: he simply hung up on her. I did the best I could at the time to deal with all of this fallout while also juggling the responsibilities of raising my young family and running our household.

My relationship with my mother during this time also became a bit strained. She and her husband had divorced, and she had yet another new boyfriend. When I went home to visit with her, my grandmother, and my aunt and uncle, it was always a battle as to where we were going to stay. She, of course, would want us to stay at her house with her and her boyfriend. It was tough because I wanted to spend time with her, but I didn't want to expose my children to someone I barely knew and wasn't sure could be trusted to be around my children. Typically, we stayed with my grandmother instead.

Eventually, I let my mother know that I would not stay with her when her boyfriend was there. I explained that I was an adult with my own family, and I would be making the choices I felt were best for my family. Something clicked during that conversation, and a new understanding bloomed between us. After all, we were both mothers.

> *Looking back, the changes she made were so helpful in repairing our relationship...*

Our relationship improved even more when she and the boyfriend broke up. She moved in with my grandmother to care for her and decided that she didn't need a man in her life. Then she became a Christian and truly realized that she could be whole without a man. Her life changed for the better, and so did our relationship. Her new outlook and our healthier, open communication strengthened our tattered bond. I felt more comfortable taking my kids to see her and allowed her to keep them for the weekend at times, so she could spend quality time with them. Looking back, the changes she made were so helpful in repairing our relationship, but motherhood was also helping me find my voice, and I was going to need it for what was to come.

Within the first four years of my marriage, I discovered that my husband struggled with sexual sin. I began to find pornography, evidence of visits to video shops, VCR tapes, and magazines hidden around the house. I didn't know the extent of what he was doing, but I knew it was bad. We began spiraling into a vicious cycle.

I truly thought each time, when he promised to stop, that would be the end of it.

I would find something disturbing and confront him, and then he would apologize and promise to stop. I would forgive him, hoping that he was sincere but also desperate to keep my family together. This cycle continued throughout our marriage. I would pull myself together after confronting him and continue on as I had a family to care for. I truly thought each time, when he promised to stop, that would be the end of it.

I always knew my husband loved our kids. He was very involved and helpful when Christian was born. After Anthony's birth, he gradually became less involved. We shared the bedtime routine for putting our kids to bed when he was home and not traveling for work. He also coached all of our kids in their various sports and stayed involved in that way. As the years went on, though, he became very disconnected. If he wasn't coaching or working, he could be found watching television or sleeping. As a husband, he was distant and disconnected. Rarely, if ever, did I feel loved or supported by him, but I had three kids to raise and was determined to do that well.

The cycle of his sexual sin continued about every six months for years, and I became increasingly numb and distant. His addiction wasn't the only issue. I was realizing that our marriage was not even remotely a partnership. I was doing everything from the shopping, cleaning, and lawn care to handling the finances. It felt like I had four children instead of three. I felt the only contribution he made was to work; thankfully he was good at his job. As the years progressed, our emotional connection faded into non-existence.

After seventeen years on autopilot, I was overcome with stress and loneliness.

After seventeen years on autopilot, I was overcome with stress and loneliness. Christian was about fifteen; Anthony was twelve; and Danie was seven. I desperately tried to keep my focus on my kids. Then I became extremely ill. I lost thirty pounds in a month and was terrified that I had cancer or some other terminal illness. I physically couldn't get out of bed. I felt horrific, and the stress was mounting over my inability to keep up with everything. I was used to running a tidy and organized household, and I just couldn't do it. I had to focus the little energy I had on caring for my kids. My husband's reaction was appalling and a huge defining moment for me. He didn't even recognize how sick I was.

One day, he found me in our laundry room overwhelmed and sobbing. He said with disdain, "What's wrong with you?" I replied, "If I don't get some help, I'm going to have a breakdown." He replied, "Well, maybe you need to delegate (the laundry) to the kids more." And then he walked away. It was then that I realized that I was living as a married woman, but, in reality, I was completely alone.

Despite my husband's insensitivity, I went to the doctor and was diagnosed with Celiac disease. This is an autoimmune disorder that causes your digestive system to produce antibodies that damage your intestines when you ingest gluten. I took on the challenge of adopting a strict, gluten-free diet and, thankfully, felt better within a month or so. I then realized that I also needed support with my mental health and started going to therapy.

I worked hard to dig in and understand and address the trauma that had such a huge impact on who I had become. My husband was indifferent to my therapy and efforts to improve myself. I learned so much about myself in therapy, but I also learned how toxic my marriage had become. My therapist helped me to see that I was my husband's enabler. I would often ask him to do something like pick up his clothes, fix something around the house, or help with the dishes, and he would agree to do it but never follow through. Regardless of the task, ultimately, I would end up doing it myself. This was a pattern in our marriage that never changed. As I started to reap the benefits of therapy myself, I began to hopefully wonder if it could be the key to saving my marriage.

I asked my husband multiple times to go to therapy for the sake of our marriage. My therapist recommended a therapist for sexual addiction for him. She advised me to give him the number to call but not to make the appointment for him. I talked to him about it, put the number on the refrigerator, and there it stayed for three years. During that time, I continued to work on myself. I wanted to do everything I possibly could to save my marriage so that, if I did have to walk away, I could do it with no regrets.

As I became healthier mentally, it became clear that he and I needed to separate. This was an excruciating decision for me. I am a Christian, and divorce was the very last option for me. I wanted my kids to have their dad, and I wanted that perfect family I had dreamt about as a little girl. I was also paralyzed by fear. I was worried about how the kids would handle us separating. I also had an irrational, yet daunting fear that he was going to kill me and my kids. Therapy helped me through that fear and taught me that I couldn't allow it to keep me from doing what was right for all of us.

> **Staying in the relationship was not only damaging to me, but it wasn't healthy for my children either.**

In addition to therapy, there was another defining moment that helped nudge me over the edge. Anthony, my middle child, was also my difficult child. Anthony and I have always had a very close relationship, but his relationship with his dad was tumultuous. One morning, I watched in silence and horror as Anthony and his dad screamed at each other in our kitchen. Seemingly frozen in that horrible moment, I finally realized that I was staying in a toxic marriage for my kids and that this was the life I was creating for them. Staying in the relationship was not only damaging to me, but it wasn't healthy for my children either. And at that point, I was positive it was not going to change. After years of suffering quiet mental abuse, I knew it was over. I was married to a man who claimed he loved me but made no effort to show it. A man who took everything I had to give but gave nothing in return. And a man who seemed void of emotion when it came to our relationship. I was empty and numb. The drive to create a better life for myself and my children was the only thing that kept me going.

I finally told my husband that we needed to separate. He was shocked and devastated and asked what he could do to save our relationship. Again, I told him he needed to go to therapy, and this time, he agreed to go. He chose to go to a pastor from church rather than the therapist that had been recommended. The pastor focused on helping him figure out what he could do for me to win my heart back. This wasn't what my husband or our relationship needed. I told him that he needed to work on himself and figure out why he was doing the things he was doing. As I got healthier, I knew in my heart that it wasn't going to work if I got healthy emotionally, and he didn't. He just couldn't understand that he needed therapy for himself, not to win my heart back. We were operating in two different worlds.

In May of that year, I gave him the deadline to move out by July. In June, he got fired, I believe on purpose so he wouldn't have to move. My newly found voice was growing stronger, and I set another deadline of the end of October for him to move out whether he had a new job or not. In early November, he moved out and began living with some friends. He continued to try to win my heart back. Suddenly, he was more than willing to mow the lawn or fix things around the house. His efforts were futile, however, because I could see that he wasn't working on himself. I knew what he was doing wasn't working and told him that, so he agreed to try a different therapist.

As soon as therapy with the new therapist got tough, he bailed out. It finally became crystal clear to me that I could not make somebody else do what they needed to do. I could only control myself. I needed to shift my focus to making the best of the situation because he was the father of my kids.

During our separation, he would come to see the kids a few nights per week to stay connected with them. Christian was seventeen, Anthony was fourteen, and Danie was nine. He would typically have dinner with them and make sure they got to bed. I made a point of making plans for those nights, so I wouldn't have to be there with him.

I wanted to see if he would do the work he needed to do to be the man, husband, and father I needed him to be. It became clear to me during this time that he was not working on himself. We had been separated for about seven months when one night, after he had been over to see the kids, I came home, got on my computer, and found a deleted email that he had been sending to a woman he wanted to hook up with. This was the final straw for me.

The next day, I made plans to file for divorce. Our divorce was amicable, and once final, we were granted shared custody of our kids. He had them every other weekend and a night during the week, and I had them the rest of the time. Although our relationship as husband and wife no longer existed, we were thankfully able to agree that we would never use our kids against each other.

Our divorce was tough on my kids primarily because we had never argued in front of them. There was no yelling and screaming; we had always fought quietly and in private. The boys may have had an idea that something was wrong because I hadn't been sleeping in the same room with my husband for probably a year and a half before the separation. They would have recognized something was off. My daughter Danie took the divorce the hardest because she was the youngest and had no idea anything had been wrong.

> **"** One of the biggest factors that impacted my personal growth was learning to forgive. **"**

Although I feel I am a completely different person today, each of the threads of this earlier life of mine shaped me. One of the biggest factors that impacted my personal growth was learning to forgive. What I've learned is that forgiveness is a process. It requires deliberate, conscious effort and must be a daily decision. Like a habit, sometimes it needs to be practiced over and over again in order to take hold. I've always been a person who tries to put myself in the shoes of others. This helps me have compassion and grace for those who have hurt me.

I know that my mother had trauma from her own childhood that impacted the decisions she made. I can also understand what it must have been like to be a single mom with no high school diploma trying to support three young children. Young and vulnerable, she stumbled into some unhealthy relationships that unfortunately negatively impacted her children. The pain caused by her choices was unintentional. I choose to share what happened to me not out of spite or disrespect for her, but in the hope that others will understand the importance of being cautious with whom they expose their children to when exploring new relationships. My mother is and has always been loving and kind. Not once have I had to wonder if she loved me. We are very close, and she is the one I turn to when things get tough. I'm proud to call her not only my mother, but my dear friend. She is greatly loved by our kids, and we all have immense love and respect for her.

My stepdad was a sick individual. I am unsure of his upbringing and the trauma that he may have endured. Forgiving him has not been as easy, and it has taken many years to get to a place where I can say I forgive him. With my oldest brother, I understood the pain and shame of abuse and the intense need to hide it. I struggle to understand the act of repeating the abuse, but I do know the pain and mental anguish it causes. Therefore, I have chosen to forgive him. I've also learned to recognize that my ex-husband experienced a lot of pain, trauma, and dysfunction in his past. This is by no means, an excuse to act out sexually or to be an emotionally distant husband, but it did give me some perspective about why he was the way he was. This helped me learn to forgive him. Again, forgiveness is a choice. It takes so much energy to stay angry and bitter and, at the end of the day, that anger and bitterness were stealing my joy. I had to choose to be an overcomer rather than a victim. Once I made that choice, forgiveness helped put me on the path to the personal growth I needed to pursue the life I longed for and deserved.

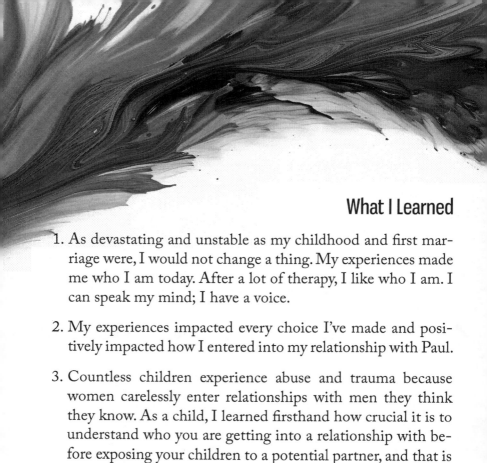

What I Learned

1. As devastating and unstable as my childhood and first marriage were, I would not change a thing. My experiences made me who I am today. After a lot of therapy, I like who I am. I can speak my mind; I have a voice.

2. My experiences impacted every choice I've made and positively impacted how I entered into my relationship with Paul.

3. Countless children experience abuse and trauma because women carelessly enter relationships with men they think they know. As a child, I learned firsthand how crucial it is to understand who you are getting into a relationship with before exposing your children to a potential partner, and that is a lesson that has consistently guided my choices as a mother.

4. God allows us to do things to help us learn important lessons. I'm glad it all happened; I have my own voice and my kids to show for it.

5. Forgiveness is an amazing thing. When you don't hold onto bitterness, negative memories and the feelings associated with them fade, and you can continue to grow as a person.

Paul

I was born in 1965 and grew up in Bay City, Michigan in a typically dysfunctional family. My parents had been married for fifty-four years when my dad passed away. Our family of four included one brother, who is three years older than me. Our parents always provided for us, but love, affection, and communication were lacking. My parents did not tell me they loved me until I was in my 40s.

As a child, I didn't have a lot of friends. I was somewhat of a loner. I was a big kid, but not very athletic. I gained a bunch of weight around third grade. My dad had taken advantage of the opportunity to buy an appliance store, and my parents' time and focus were 100% devoted to that. As a result of the dysfunction in my family, I had become a closet eater, and the fact that nobody was monitoring my behavior at home contributed to my weight gain.

> " I didn't truly understand the damaging impact this had on me until I went to therapy much later in life. "

My parents started working together and being together 24-7. It really took a toll on their relationship and our family. Among the few memories I have of that time, those of my parents having knock-down, drag-out fights hurling various objects across rooms at each other stand out most. They had both grown up in dysfunctional families themselves, and there was a lot of unresolved anger that they brought into their relationship. As a family, we rarely spoke and showed very little affection towards one another. I didn't truly understand the damaging impact this had on me until I went to therapy much later in life.

As part of that therapy, I participated in *Eye Movement Desensitization Reprocessing Therapy* (EMDR) which helps bring memories and the negative or traumatic feelings associated with them to the surface so that new, more positive, feelings can be attached to the memories. This process is meant to allow the negative associations with the memory to be desensitized and create a better sense of well-being around the trauma that has occurred. Even with this therapy, my memories are few. One thing I do recall is sitting in the front row of our Catholic church every Sunday as a kid; to onlookers, we were a healthy, happy, and devout family.

Since we rarely communicated or showed emotion in my family, my relationship with my brother as we were growing up was distant. In the years leading up to and during middle school, I spent most of my time at home alone. My parents were working six days per week until at least 6:30 p.m. most nights, and my brother was either with his girlfriend or busy with sports. I mastered the art of cooking pizza and macaroni and cheese for dinner and focused on getting good grades. Neither of my parents had gone to college, so they stressed the importance of getting good grades. They wanted us to have that opportunity. They instilled a great work ethic in me. When I turned twelve, I started working at the appliance store with my parents and my brother. Working there with them made me feel important. It also helped me understand what they did at work, and I learned that I liked making money.

My brother and I got closer when I was in late middle school going into high school. He was very good at sports, and I followed in his footsteps. Everything changed when I went to high school. I had become taller, leaner, and more comfortable in my own skin. I became more self-assured and was catching up to my brother athletically. We both excelled in school and did well in sports, which strengthened our bond and paved the way for our football careers in college.

My brother had a great freshman year playing football before injuring his Achilles tendon. Unfortunately, this side-tracked his football career. He never started after that injury. College for me was a time to thrive. I maintained an A-B average at The College of Wooster in Ohio and excelled at football. My parents were very supportive when it came to sports, and they came to most of my games. My brother would also visit and come to three or four of my games per year. We developed a much stronger bond during this time.

I had also started connecting more with girls. I fell hard for my second girlfriend in college. This was the first time that I felt a strong emotional connection with a girl. That connection was shattered when she slept with my college roommate and sent me back into my shell. I decided I didn't ever want a family or children. Deep down, I knew I was messed up, so why would I want to create and mess up kids of my own?

As a young adult, I made a vow to myself to remain emotionally disconnected. This didn't stop me from dating many women and seeking acceptance and comfort through sexual gratification. I just kept my distance emotionally. If things started to get serious with one of them, I bolted. I also found myself striving to be the guy that everybody wanted to be around, the guy that everybody loved. I know now that this required a great deal of acting and energy since I didn't even truly know or like myself.

My 1st Marriage

I met my first wife when I was twenty-four. She was thirty-one and had two children from her first marriage. The youngest was seven, and the oldest was nine. We dated for three or four months, but I quickly realized that I had no desire to have an instant family with step kids. I had started dating someone else, but somehow ended up hooking up again with her, and she got pregnant. She left a message on my answering machine sharing the shocking news. Ironically, my girlfriend at the time was standing beside me when I played the life-altering message that day. It was splitsville for us very shortly after that!

Looking back, I was extremely self-centered at this time. I let my ex know that the pregnancy was her issue to deal with, not mine. I was in complete denial. In my mind, I was happily dating someone else, and I assumed she would have an abortion. She didn't. And that someone else didn't stick around.

> *When my first daughter, Ashley, was born, everything changed for me.*

My ex and I didn't speak much at all until she was five months into the pregnancy. She finally convinced me to go to counseling with her because we weren't getting along and had a child on the way. My first experience with that counselor sparked a transformation in me. It was as simple as the therapist asking me if I wanted to be a father. Hearing that question verbalized caused a dramatic shift in my psyche. I started to support her at that point and even went to Lamaze with her. We recommitted to treating each other with respect and kindness for the rest of her pregnancy. When my first daughter, Ashley, was born, everything changed for me.

I spent as much time as I possibly could with Ashley, even though her mom and I were not together. Once Ashley was six weeks old, I began functioning as a single parent. I vividly recall the first time I took her home with me. I timidly handled the diaper bag and newborn and fumbled with the car seat. When we got to my place, I didn't have a crib, so I put her on my bed with blankets and towels around her. I stayed up carefully watching her all night, and it dawned on me that I had no idea what I was doing. I had never taken care of kids of any age. Thankfully, I had a roommate who helped me learn the ropes when it came to infant care. Ultimately, the love I felt for my newborn daughter was enough to override all the discomfort and difficulty that came with being a clueless new father.

Becoming a father immediately and completely changed me for the better. My life had been all about me up until that point. My friends changed as I stopped partying, and I became a Christian. A woman I knew had invited me to church, and I started going faithfully. Although my relationship with my baby's mother had improved upon Ashley's arrival, I knew I didn't want to be with her. I continued to date other women, and she lived with some other guy. Since we had a child together, we had to be in constant communication, and this inevitably strengthened our relationship.

"
This division of these important roles contributed to our dysfunction as a couple and as parents.
"

After two years of co-parenting, we had grown closer, and eventually, we proclaimed our love for each other. We decided to get married when Ashley was three years old. Her two boys became my stepchildren, and I was suddenly responsible for a family of five. I know now that the marriage was partially out of obligation and partially a result of my distorted view of what love was. I loved not being alone, and I loved the idea of being a good father and having a family. Should we have gotten married? Probably not. But we did. It is part of my story, and I'm glad it happened.

We had a few good years of marriage. As a parent, I was what you might call a Disneyland dad. I wanted to provide and have all the fun that comes with having kids, but I wasn't interested in the other parts of parenting. I played the role of the fun parent, and my ex-wife was the disciplinarian. This division of these important roles contributed to our dysfunction as a couple and as parents. As it turned out, no amount of fun could neutralize the dysfunction.

I had an explosive temper, and so did my wife. Looking back, I was not in a good place as a husband, father, or person. Unbeknownst to my spouse, I increasingly turned to pornography and visits to strip clubs searching for some sense of comfort and control. Those feelings were fleeting and dissipated as soon as I returned to the reality of my marriage. What I remember most is the fighting. We argued constantly, and often arguments exploded into yelling and screaming fights. As they say, unhealthy attracts unhealthy, and we were a few years and three kids deep into an extremely unhealthy relationship. Looking back, four or five fights in a day would be a good day in my first marriage. I don't think Jeannette and I have had more than five disagreements in over sixteen years of marriage. My current reality accentuates just how volatile my first marriage truly was. It was like riding a roller coaster, with wild highs and lows, with seemingly no warning or reason. When we'd hit a low, I just held on until we started to climb towards that next high again.

A great high in that increasingly tumultuous time of my life was the birth of my second daughter, Mariah. As our family grew, I also became more successful professionally. I had started running a business with a partner. We had great success very quickly and made a lot of money. My wife and I purchased a 40-acre ranch with cows, chickens, and horses. We were extremely blessed when it came to finances; that was one thing we never had to worry about. I was in my thirties and proudly balancing the roles of husband, father, and successful businessman. We were also able to do some traveling and have fun as a family. To any outsider, it may have looked like I was a man who had it all.

> Despite all we had, we still did not have a healthy relationship.

Despite all we had, we still did not have a healthy relationship. I realize now that my ex-wife had a lot of baggage from her past that she brought into our marriage. Her father had died when she was just ten, and she was physically abused by her mother. She had also been abused in her first marriage. I had grown up extremely lonely and lacking an emotional connection with my parents. I had been the emotional equivalent of a twelve-year-old looking for a mother figure when I got married. We were a toxic combination from the start. One of the biggest things I have learned that I cannot stress enough is that when you are unhealthy and in pursuit of a relationship, you will attract others who are unhealthy. Now, when I counsel or mentor guys, I always say that the number one priority when looking for a significant other is emotional health.

Although my first wife and I fought all the time, a few major events led to the actual destruction of our marriage. First, my business failed overnight. My partner and I lost eighty percent of our income in three weeks. We went from making a boatload of cash to making nothing. I didn't have a lot of money saved at the time either. My partner generously gave me $100,000 to walk away; it was truly a gift because he knew I didn't have anything saved. I then got another job earning about a third of what I had previously made. My wife and I could no longer afford the lifestyle we had become used to. This would have been difficult for a healthy couple to handle, and healthy we were not. I woke up one day to the reality that I was in way over my head with a wife I couldn't get along with, issues with sexual addiction, two biological children, two stepchildren, and major financial issues. My wife's boys went to live with their dad, which enraged her further. Her behavior became more unpredictable, and any stability she had previously exhibited disappeared.

Things became even more difficult when I had to have knee surgery and developed a severe bone infection afterward. I was unable to work and was in the hospital off and on for two months, facing the possibility of a leg amputation. This was a major additional stressor on our marriage, which was already speeding downhill fast.

After I had recovered from my medical crisis, we began a cycle of separating and getting back together. I had been living a secret life and struggling with sexual addiction for years. I realized during my marital turmoil that I had been living one life as a Christian husband and father, and one as a sexual addict. My wife had no idea. I was learning that just like any addiction, mine had the power to destroy me. I knew I couldn't go on that way and our marriage didn't stand a chance if I did, so I sought therapy. I made a conscious choice to do the work to get better. Aware that my wife would have a difficult time understanding my addiction and supporting my recovery, I kept my therapy a secret from her as well.

> "As I recovered, I was less angry and combative. These changes in my personality didn't fit into the pattern of conflict that defined our marriage."

I was away on a business trip when my wife discovered some of my recovery books and journals at home. She called to confront me, and I had no choice but to reveal the details of the dual life I'd been living. This revelation started our cycle of separating and getting back together. Of course, the secret of my addiction was damaging to our relationship. But there was also fallout from my recovery. Rather than being relieved or supportive of my efforts to change, she seemed to grow angrier and more resentful as I grew healthier. As I recovered, I was less angry and combative. These changes in my personality didn't fit into the pattern of conflict that defined our marriage.

We had been back together after one of our separations for a few weeks when I came home from a business trip to find an empty house. Our wedding album was cut up into a million pieces on the living room floor, and everything and everyone was gone. She had wiped out our bank accounts and maxed out the credit cards. I literally had twenty bucks in my pocket, half a tank of gas, and a bunch of animals to feed. To make matters worse, I didn't know where she had taken my kids. I was devastated. I laid down in our living room crying out to God in pain and desperation with my face pressed into our Berber carpet. To this day, I can't stand the touch or feel of Berber carpeting.

As painful as that day was, it was one of the most important days of my life because it humbled me and showed me that I still had work to do on myself. My ex-wife eventually reached out with a text message a few weeks later and told me where she was staying. I was extremely relieved when we were able to make arrangements for me to pick up the kids and spend a day with them. When I went to pick them up, she had worked herself up into a fury. As I stood in the doorway trying to talk to her, she hurled a shoe at me and broke the window in her door. I grabbed my shell-shocked kids and got out of there as quickly as I could.

Our relationship continued to deteriorate from there. We had been separated for a year and a half before I knew our marriage was truly over. I recall exactly where I was standing in the house, we'd previously shared when she called and told me in the nastiest possible way that she was sleeping with another man. I filed for divorce, and a grueling process and custody battle ensued. We were all swept up in a whirlwind of emotional proceedings that culminated with a trial. Several strangers were recruited and became entangled in our very personal drama including child advocates, child psychologists, and a Guardian ad litem for the girls. Of course, each of us had our own attorney. All these individuals needed to be paid, and since my ex-wife had no money, I paid for it all. The total for my divorce was over $100,000 when all was said and done.

> It was a painful and confusing time for them, so my focus shifted to bettering myself and living for them.

During the divorce process, I continued the hard work of getting my life back on track. I sold the ranch and all of our animals and moved into an apartment near my ex's house in the mountains outside of Denver. This was my attempt to be close to them in case they needed anything and make things easier on our kids. My new home had a wood stove and no air-conditioning. It was vastly different from the ranch I had just sold, but my life was substantially more peaceful. The relationship between my girls and their mother was strained to say the least. It was a painful and confusing time for them, so my focus shifted to bettering myself and living for them.

It's difficult to put into words what an incredibly difficult time it was for all of us. My ex had been taking prescription pain medication and drinking before she left, but she had gotten more heavily into drugs and alcohol since. Her temper and behavior had become even more violent. During one of Ashley's counseling sessions, she shared that her mother had been violent with her. The very next day there was a court hearing, and that was it. I was suddenly granted full custody of the girls. A plan was put in place for me to pick them up. Part of that plan was that the sheriff would meet me at her house, but he didn't show up. When I arrived, she was hiding behind the door and jumped out and sucker-punched me. After the shock wore off, all I could think about was how unstable she had become and how grateful I was to have custody of our kids. Although I was suffering myself, I put a great deal of energy into shielding them from her instability and attempted to be strong for them.

After things settled down a bit, I still let the girls see their mother. Everything I had read and heard in parenting classes advised allowing children to continue some sort of relationship with the parent who didn't have custody regardless of the circumstances. At first, Ashley and Mariah had supervised visits with her. This was disastrous. The girls couldn't really connect with her, and she would say nasty things about and to the supervisor during the visits. Eventually, I allowed the girls to go to her house unsupervised. Ashley would have short visits, but never stayed overnight. Mariah was younger and wanted to spend more time with her. She would stay overnight at times. The damage those visits and my ex-wife's mental instability caused to my daughters was sometimes evident when they came home, but some deeper wounds remained hidden until years later.

To this day, this is a weight that is difficult to bear as a father. When I think of those dark days, I'm haunted by the memory of a phone call on Ashley's sixteenth birthday. It was her mother, who proceeded to tell my daughter that she wished she'd never had her, and that she was no longer her daughter. I'm filled with sorrow, fury, and regret when I think about that call. It was one of several moments that I should have protected my daughters and cut off all contact with my ex. I was so beaten down and exhausted from being in constant conflict with her that I gave in to her demands to see them. I wish I had done a better job of shielding them from their mother.

Despite the ongoing drama with her, I wanted to focus on the opportunity to raise my daughters and be the best father I could possibly be. I knew I needed help, so I sought support through a divorce recovery class in church. The teacher of the class started by explaining to the group that it was not a hook-up class. Ironically, she and I hooked up. I ended up dating her for a while. Overall, it was a good relationship and really what I needed at the time. My ex-wife had been so mentally abusive, degrading, and mean throughout our marriage and as it was ending. My new girlfriend was kind and great at filling me up, and she was great with my kids. As we became more serious, I discovered that she was an emotional wreck with a lot of insecurities. She was the definition of emotionally needy. She needed to constantly hear how beautiful she was and always feel needed. It didn't work out. And I'm so glad it didn't.

After the relationship ended, I created a profile on *Match.com*. I met nineteen women on *Match*. What I quickly realized was that they were all very attractive on the outside, but bitter and angry on the inside. Many of them had been cheated on, but they were still looking for a man to fulfill them. I ended up dating only two of them.

One of the women I dated was a forty-two-year-old millionaire who had never been married. She was appealing to me because I wanted to be taken care of; again, I was looking for that motherly nurturing and emotional connection that I never had as a child. I was also seriously considering going back to school for a degree in counseling, and she was more than capable of taking care of me financially. She had some issues of her own, however. The deal-breaker with her was that my kids couldn't stand her. Mariah later told me, "I liked that she bought me clothes, but other than that, I'm glad you didn't marry her."

The other woman I dated was also very successful, but it didn't work out with her either. She was extremely insecure and jealous of my relationship with my kids. Although these relationships didn't work out, they were an important part of my journey because they helped me learn more about what I did and didn't want and need in a partner.

What I Learned

1. Like Jeannette, I have no regrets about my childhood or my first marriage. I know I wasn't a great parent early on, but I learned from my mistakes. In working to heal, overcome my addiction, forgive myself and forgive others, I became the best person, spouse, stepdad, and parent I can be.

2. We can't blame our parents. Chances are your parents are messed up because their parents were messed up. The cycle can and does continue unless you do the hard work to interrupt it.

3. Here's the reality: we are all *jacked up*. The beauty is that, despite traumatic childhoods and failed marriages, you can still find happiness, success, and fulfillment. The key is doing the work to become emotionally healthy.

4. Until healing takes place, starting a new relationship, no matter how wonderful you might think the other person is, will not work to fix what is broken.

5. Marriage is work and so is parenting— but both can and should be fulfilling and beautiful. Co-existing in a constant state of conflict is fruitless and damaging to all involved.

two

The Magic of Therapy

*"Trauma creates change you don't choose. Healing is
about creating the change you do choose."*
Michelle Rosenthal

Paul

The first time I ever went to therapy, I was in college. I had a girlfriend who tried to commit suicide, not once, but twice in the same week. She had written me a goodbye letter blaming me for her despair and hopelessness. The therapist was great; she did a wonderful job of assuring me that the situation was not my fault and that my girlfriend had issues that were beyond my control. That was all I wanted and needed (or thought I needed) at that time.

During my first marriage, my ex-wife and I went to counseling a few times together. Couples therapy didn't go well with her because of her intrusive insecurity. She always thought the therapists favored me over her, so we could never really make progress. Most of our time was spent playing the blame game, and she did most of the blaming. I can't say I was *all in*, either. I truly wanted peace in my marriage, but being *all in* would have required me to be more open and honest with her and with myself about my addiction than I was willing to be at that point.

Early on, as our marriage began spiraling out of control, I wasn't closed off to the idea of therapy. In fact, I was beginning to realize it was something that I truly needed. There was a Christian group called *The Promise Keepers* that did stadium events all over the United States. The head football coach at the University of Colorado, Boulder had founded it. With the primary goal of helping men apply set principles based upon scripture to their lives. It became very successful and grew in size and popularity quickly. They eventually published a magazine called *New Man*. In it, I came across an article that resonated with me. The article was about a man who was living a dual life. He had unresolved issues from his past that were causing him to act out sexually, but at the same time, he was a Christian and a loving husband and father. I thought as I read it: "This guy is describing me. I need help." The author was a therapist in Colorado Springs.

I called to schedule a therapy session and ended up seeing his business partner instead. I immediately connected with him. He seemed to understand me and wanted to nurture my ability to have successful relationships. What makes him so effective is his understanding of the hearts and souls of men. I began seeing him while I was married and saw him consistently after my first marriage collapsed. I would go every other week for six months or so. Then I would stop going unless I felt I needed to see him. He has been supporting me on and off throughout the last twenty-one years. I've seen him over a hundred times, and I still go see him today when something comes up that induces anxiety that I know I can't manage on my own.

My therapist introduced me to the concept of *EMDR or Eye Movement Desensitization Reprogramming*. This is an amazing tool that I think of as cognitive therapy on steroids. It is designed to help dissolve stress associated with traumatic memories and train the brain to reformulate negative beliefs. It helps you dig deeply into the wounds of your past and bring them to the surface so that you can heal. After learning about it, I saw another counselor when I started this process because my therapist wasn't yet doing it. In all my experiences with therapy, EMDR was the thing that really opened my eyes to who I am, and why I've done the things I've done. It's truly helped me heal from some deep childhood wounds.

One of the other things that my therapist taught me about is something called, *The Wound, The Vow, and The Lie*. This can be used universally for men and women. For me, my wound was that there was no apparent love and affection expressed within my family when I was growing up. This caused me to vow to be somebody that everyone would love. The lie within all of this was that I could never be somebody that everyone would love, so my vow was not realistic or healthy. Identifying the lie and my flawed vow helped me understand what I needed to do to begin healing.

My therapist and these revelations eventually helped me understand how much I wanted and needed to hear my dad tell me that he loved me before he died. With my therapist's guidance, I went through the process of crafting a letter to my father, asking for him to tell me that he loved me and was proud of me. I had a deep, painful wound buried within me that stemmed from never hearing those words from him.

I sent that letter, fully believing that there would never be a response. I remember in vibrant detail the day that he called and the sound of his voice. He was, as always, brief and direct, "I got your letter. Of course I love you, and I'm proud of you." That was it. I had one meaningful conversation with my dad my entire life, and it lasted less than two minutes. I now mentor men with obvious wounds who have never heard even that. I had to learn that this was all my dad was emotionally capable of, and when I did, a huge weight lifted from my shoulders, and the healing began. I am now at peace with my relationship with my dad.

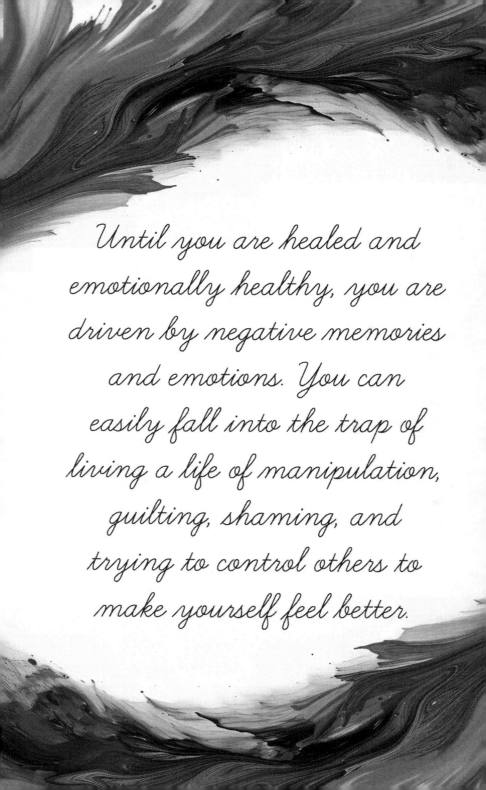

Until you are healed and
emotionally healthy, you are
driven by negative memories
and emotions. You can
easily fall into the trap of
living a life of manipulation,
guilting, shaming, and
trying to control others to
make yourself feel better.

After I'd worked on myself and started dating again, red flags would pop up all the time. I would know immediately when I was talking to someone who had not dealt with her past. Before therapy, I would date women based solely on their looks, even if I knew they weren't good people. After therapy, my paradigm shifted. I would go to meet someone at *Starbucks* and think, *she's hot*. But then she would open her mouth, and it was one red flag after another. When I became the new, healthier version of myself, those red flags guided my decisions more than the outward appearances of the women I met. Lucky for me, Jeannette was both beautiful and emotionally healthy!

Jeannette and I did premarital counseling with my therapist, and we've seen him a few other times as a couple. I'm a firm believer in therapy and that everyone needs it. We all have wounds that shape our paradigm or worldview. Until you work on yourself, you truly cannot be in a healthy and meaningful relationship with anyone else. That applies to all types of relationships: romantic relationships, friendships, parental-child relationships, and professional relationships.

Until you are healed and emotionally healthy, you are driven by negative memories and emotions. You can easily fall into the trap of living a life of manipulation, guilting, shaming, and trying to control others to make yourself feel better. But you never feel better for long. Therapy helps you shift your view of yourself and the world. It teaches you that the negative things that have happened in your life are not all everybody else's fault, and they are not all your fault. They happened, and ultimately, you need to take the steps to begin healing from them; you are the only one who can. Part of that process involves forgiving the people who have wronged you and moving on. I don't necessarily buy into the phrase *forgive and forget* because you don't really forget. You just learn to let go of things, and they gradually fade into your background. When you don't have those negative memories at the forefront of your life, they can no longer rob you of true happiness.

So many people want to do couples therapy, and that's great, but I would encourage them to do individual therapy first. Work on yourselves first, and then come together and work on being a couple. If you start with couples therapy, it often just turns into the blame game. If you work on yourself first, you learn to understand why you have the feelings you do, and why you do the things you do.

For me, it came back to my dad never listening to me when I was a kid. That caused many issues for me that had nothing to do with the other people in my relationships. It was all about me and how I learned to be and react as a child. How we react to things in our adult lives is how we learned to react as children. I have learned that our paradigms are shaped between the ages of five and sixteen. So, until you heal from any trauma that occurred during that period in your life, you will react to things the way you would have at that age (between five and sixteen). It's so true. I saw it in myself before therapy, and I see it all the time in the business world. If you've never learned how to effectively manage your emotional responses to things, that will spill over into your relationships.

It's interesting because so many people think that things that happened to them long ago don't matter. The problem is that trauma shifts your psyche. It's like you literally are walking through life with a skewed perspective, and you don't even realize it. It doesn't necessarily have to be deep trauma like physical or sexual abuse, either. Many people are like me and grew up with parents who never told us they loved us and were proud of us. I hear that from many of the men that I work with who struggle with sexual addiction just as I had. So, you do one of two things: you become passive and act out emotionally, or you become like I was and operate from this intense desire to make everybody love you. You do that because it makes you feel better about yourself. But that feeling is fleeting.

This is why I believe that individual therapy needs to happen first. It is ninety percent of what you need, and the rest you can work on together as a couple. So much of developing a healthy relationship is about what you bring forth into the relationship. If you haven't done therapy individually, you go from one relationship to another, carrying your baggage with you. It becomes incredibly easy to blame the other person—much easier than really doing the hard work of self-reflection and transforming negative thoughts and bad habits into positive ones. As difficult as that work can be, it truly is transformative. During my own recovery journey, I started a men's group for men struggling with sexual addiction just as I had. My work with these men confirmed just how transformative working toward emotional health can be. That group is still flourishing today, after twenty-two years.

Therapy has made me a different person. I mean, I'm a pretty happy and funny guy. That's my personality. I'm an extrovert, and I enjoy what I do. That hasn't changed, but what has changed is how I look at relationships with people, even people I have just met. Before therapy, I would be thinking, *Well, what can I get from this relationship? What can I get from this person?* Now, I think about what I can give the other person or help him or her with. I view conversations and connections with people differently. I'm always thinking about what I can do to make that other person's life better. I think people sense and appreciate that.

> *You can change in dramatically positive ways with the help of therapy.*

Another way I have changed is that I no longer have that raging temper. Before, I could be happy and loving 90% of the time, but if something set me off, I'd be in a state of instant fury. I would slam doors, throw, and break things, yell and scream—anything to quickly and violently release my anger. As a result of therapy, I think I've been angry enough to raise my voice maybe four times in the past twenty years.

Looking back at my first marriage, if I had a major meltdown only four times in a week, that was a small miracle. Sometimes people will say, "I can't have that or change in that way; that's not my personality." I disagree. You *can* change in dramatically positive ways with the help of therapy. Jeannette and I have both experienced this kind of change in our lives.

Our experiences with therapy have led us down the path of mentoring others. I mentor men who have had some of the same struggles I did, and Jeannette works with women who have suffered in relationships damaged by sexual addiction. We have mentored couples together and have also worked with couples doing premarital counseling. Premarital counseling is interesting because things look so different once you are married. When you're dating and things are going well, you answer all the questions very positively. You're in love, and life is good. The answers sometimes start to shift with the ups and downs of married life, especially when you are merging families. The behaviors of addicts also ebb and flow. When relationships are fresh, fun, and new, there is no need to seek comfort by acting out sexually. When things become challenging, those destructive behaviors naturally increase.

Others that we know or work with who recognize a need for therapy sometimes are resistant for various reasons. When I encourage some of the guys I work with to pursue therapy, they investigate the cost and become very hesitant. My response is always, "Would you rather have a failed marriage and go through a divorce that will cost you about 100 grand?" Investing in therapy is a lot like putting gas in a car. Just as you need gas to make a car run, you need therapy to make your life run smoothly.

Another barrier that will sometimes come up is the stigma around therapy. The fear of admitting there might be something wrong with you can be debilitating. Our answer for that: there is something wrong with all of us! Remember? We are all jacked up in some way.

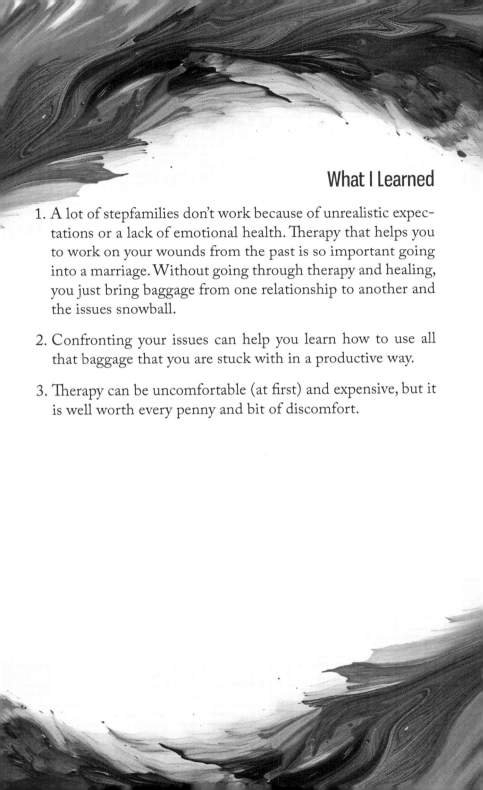

What I Learned

1. A lot of stepfamilies don't work because of unrealistic expectations or a lack of emotional health. Therapy that helps you to work on your wounds from the past is so important going into a marriage. Without going through therapy and healing, you just bring baggage from one relationship to another and the issues snowball.

2. Confronting your issues can help you learn how to use all that baggage that you are stuck with in a productive way.

3. Therapy can be uncomfortable (at first) and expensive, but it is well worth every penny and bit of discomfort.

Jeannette

I don't remember a particular event in my first marriage that made me realize I needed therapy. Over time, I came to the realization my marriage was a mess, and so was I. I needed help processing my emotions and feelings. Up until that point, I had lived my whole life trying to please others. I have always been extremely sensitive and loyal, so I never expressed my opinions, feelings, or needs. I had carried the trauma I endured as a child into my adulthood and my first marriage. Eventually, I could no longer stuff my feelings and act like I was okay. Before starting therapy, I didn't know who I was or what I needed. I felt like I was drowning in quicksand. I was doing everything I could to keep my head from going under and struggling just to survive. I felt completely empty and alone. I knew things needed to change, and therapy was the lifeline I needed.

> **"**
> *Therapy helped me understand how much the trauma I endured as a child had left me feeling insecure and unsure of myself as an adult.*
> **"**

Therapy helped me understand how much the trauma I endured as a child had left me feeling insecure and unsure of myself as an adult. I thought, *I'll just be the wall-flower and fade into the background. I don't want anybody noticing me, and I don't want to cause any trouble, I don't want to rock that boat.* That's how I ended up being in my first marriage and staying in it for so long. I had to learn about the impact that trauma had on me and how it impacted the choices I made. Without those understandings, I might still be barely surviving in an unhealthy marriage.

At the beginning of my therapy journey, I worked intensely on dealing with the abuse that I had gone through as a child. I realized I had a lot of shame from what had happened to me and believed that I would cause problems in our family if I shared what had happened. As a result, I kept it a secret into my early

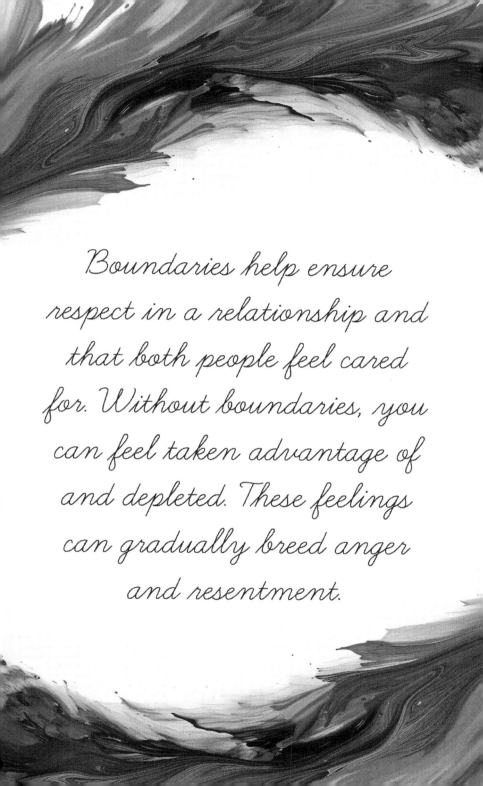

Boundaries help ensure respect in a relationship and that both people feel cared for. Without boundaries, you can feel taken advantage of and depleted. These feelings can gradually breed anger and resentment.

thirties. Acknowledging the sexual abuse that I had endured in my young life and talking about it was the first step in healing. I learned that it was not my fault and nothing I did caused this to happen to me. I realized being sexually abused does not have to define my life, and I gradually learned how to overcome what happened to me.

A life-changing component of my therapy was learning to set boundaries, which I had never done. I was a people pleaser and knew that setting boundaries could displease others. I learned that boundaries are an integral component of any healthy relationship. Boundaries help ensure respect in a relationship and that both people feel cared for. Without boundaries, you can feel taken advantage of and depleted. These feelings can gradually breed anger and resentment. That was me. Setting boundaries was extremely difficult for me. I never wanted to hurt anyone or be mean; I've always been very sensitive to how others feel. I needed guidance in finding that line. I needed someone else to tell me, "It's okay to take what you need. You don't have to live in misery." That someone was my therapist.

For me, therapy was a place where I felt heard and validated. I had never really experienced that before. It helped me understand that I wasn't crazy. In the beginning, I would have a jumbled mess of emotions and feelings that I couldn't make sense of. After my therapy sessions, I would leave with clarity and direction. It felt like I was finally out of the quicksand and on the beach, able to breathe and rest. I was no longer struggling to stay alive. Unfortunately, my ex-husband remained trapped in the sand.

While we were married, my ex-husband never got the amount or type of therapy he needed. He chose to quit going when things got tough. I learned that he had some major trauma and secrets from his past that he was in complete denial about. As soon as he was confronted with the opportunity to really dig into those issues, he stopped going to therapy altogether. Ultimately, he was willing to walk away from his marriage and his kids because he was afraid to confront those issues. He had never had to deal with any of those feelings, and he never learned to do so. There are so many people out there suffering like my ex-husband. When the going gets tough, they bail. It's like the wounds are so deep and so raw that they cannot fathom bringing the issues to the surface. So, they remain stuck, sometimes for their entire lives.

I'm indescribably grateful that therapy helped me put things into perspective and realize that my thoughts and feelings have value. I learned to set boundaries, and I learned to forgive. I spent four years on and off seeing my therapist. I went very consistently at first, and it wasn't cheap. We didn't have a lot of money at the time; we were living payday to payday. The sessions were expensive, but it was worth every penny. It's hard for me to agree when people say they don't have money for therapy. Money was tight for me when I started, but I decided that I wanted to be healthy, happy, and the best I could be for myself and my loved ones, so I found a way to make it work. I had to give up other things, but I was determined not to give up therapy because I knew it was a big and necessary step towards a healthier and happier life. It was my key to becoming the best possible version of myself, and it was so worth it.

I am not the same person that I was prior to therapy. I have strength that I never knew I had. I am free to express my thoughts and feelings. I know I am valuable and have so much to contribute to my relationships and the world. I have learned to accept what has happened to me. The abuse, my unstable childhood, and my divorce have made me a better person because I have chosen to allow God to use it for good in my life. I am not a victim; I am an overcomer. My experiences have made me who I am today. For me, it was empowering to realize that I am a strong, capable, and intelligent woman. Today, I am out of the quicksand, off the beach, and free to roam in an open field of wildflowers. I am enjoying an amazing life with an amazing life partner.

In my relationship with Paul, I'm not afraid to say what I think or express my feelings. I'm willing to stand up and disagree when necessary. We don't have a lot of conflict, but when we do, we are able to have a healthy discussion and come to a resolution. We respect each other. I'm proud of who I am and of the work that I did to get here. I believe Paul and I have a good marriage because we have each done the work to deal with our issues. Therapy changed both of our lives for the better. We both committed to that work, and as a result, we have been blessed with a great marriage and a beautiful family.

What I Learned

1. Therapy takes work. It is hard, but it is so worth it.

2. My wound was that I grew up without stability or a father. My vow was to grow up and have a perfect family of my own. My lie was that nothing is perfect, and there must be a strong and healthy commitment on both sides to have a lasting relationship.

3. My childhood doesn't have to define me. I am not a victim; I am an overcomer.

4. Forgiveness is crucial in the healing process. Bitterness keeps you from moving forward.

5. God will always use my pain for good.

6. Here is the bottom line: if you are going into a second or third marriage, it is imperative to work on your stuff from the past first. If you don't, you are just going to re-traumatize yourself and your kids. It becomes this never-ending cycle of trauma until you deal with your past and heal. The issues will continue to snowball because you'll carry the wounds from your childhood and the previous marriage(s) into the new relationships. We see so many people who go into a relationship looking for the other person to fulfill them, and unfortunately, that doesn't work. To truly thrive as an individual, partner, and parent, commit to working on yourself first. You won't regret it!

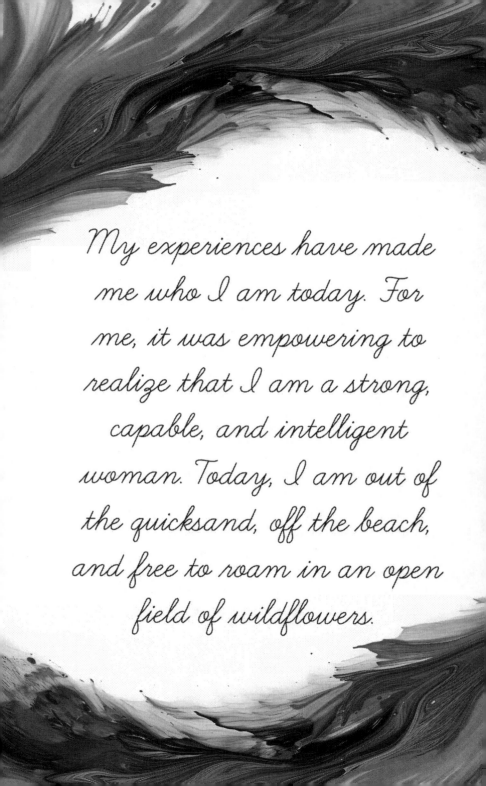

My experiences have made me who I am today. For me, it was empowering to realize that I am a strong, capable, and intelligent woman. Today, I am out of the quicksand, off the beach, and free to roam in an open field of wildflowers.

three

New Beginnings

"The direction you choose to face determines whether you're standing at the end or the beginning of a road."
– Richelle E. Goodrich

Jeannette

After my divorce, as I began to really heal, I remember writing about the kind of person I would want to be with should I ever pursue a relationship again in the back of a book. At the top of the list was a man who had kids and was a good role model and father. He needed to have integrity and be good with his money. There could be absolutely no infidelity in his history. He also needed to be a Christian and a strong believer.

I was forty years old, divorced, and ready to think about pursuing a new, healthy, but casual relationship. With my list of ideal qualities in mind, I created a profile on *Match.com*. That's where I connected with Paul. We chatted for about two weeks on *Match* before talking on the phone. I was immediately impressed by and endeared to him because of the way he handled a request to talk on the phone. He gave me his full name, the name of his workplace, and his work phone number. He told me I could call to verify that he was really who he said he was because he wanted me to feel safe giving out my number. There was an unspoken cautiousness that he, intuitively as a parent, understood. That was incredibly comforting for me because I had been very leery about meeting somebody online and about bringing someone new into our lives in general. This wasn't just about me; I had three children to consider. I ended up giving my number to him, and when we talked, I became more intrigued by him and our potential relationship.

Paul and I had very serious conversations and opened up to each other very quickly. When he asked me what led to my divorce, I shared some of the details about my ex-husband's sexual addiction. He shared that he had struggled with the same type of addiction and that he was in his fifth year of recovery. Initially, I thought to myself, *What is going on? Does every single man in America struggle with this?* Internally, I fought the urge to flee. As he continued to share the details of his addiction, his failed marriage, and his relationship with God, I could tell he was different. I was so attracted to his honesty and openness and so grateful that he was giving me all the information I needed to make an informed decision about whether or not to pursue a relationship with him.

After several conversations, I was comfortable enough to agree to meet in person and go to lunch with him. He later shared that he had taken several women out for dinner before he met me and had decided that it was a colossal waste of money. He had started meeting them at *Starbucks* instead. I knew I was special because he took me to *Chipotle* for our first date. It was quite an upgrade! We were there for three hours and talked non-stop the entire time. How I felt sitting and talking with him for the first time was indescribable; it felt nothing like a first meeting. I left our first date feeling very connected to and interested in him. I had been hoping to find some companionship and to be able to go to a movie or out to dinner when my kids were with their dad, and he seemed like he might be that perfect, comfortable fit. In no way was I looking to get maried again, though.

Paul

I was the opposite. I wanted to meet someone special and build a healthy relationship. I wanted a life partner and to be married again. Oddly enough, I had also created a list of desirable characteristics for the perfect companion. In the back of my bible, I had written down twelve things I wanted in a woman, including specifics like hair color and height. Near the top of my list was that this woman had to have kids and be willing to accept my kids. The number one characteristic I was searching for was someone with emotional stability. I mentor a lot of men who are getting remarried, and one of the things they always say they want is to marry a Christian. I tend to say, "Well, that's nice, but emotional stability absolutely needs to come first." Because of what I had been through with my first wife, this was a no-brainer for me.

I knew when Jeannette walked into Chipotle for that first meeting that I was going to marry her. She radiated with outer and inner beauty, and she was nothing like the other women I had been meeting. Our conversation flowed easily, and we discovered that we had so much in common. We *did* have our second date at Starbucks, and we shared our first kiss in that parking lot. As our relationship grew, we spent countless hours on the phone getting to know each other deeply.

> **"** *We really dug deep early because of everything we'd both been through, but also because we knew there was something special in front of us worth pursuing* **"**

At the time, Jeannette didn't have a cellphone plan with unlimited minutes and had started to rack up huge bills. I bought her a cellphone and put her on my plan so that we could talk as long as we wanted to. And boy did we talk! As Jeannette shared, we really dug deep early because of everything we'd both been through, but also because we knew there was something special in front of us worth pursuing. We dove into conversations about the importance of emotional health and the work we'd both done to make ourselves better.

Looking back, I still feel incredibly lucky to have found someone who checked virtually every box on that list I'd created in my bible: someone I could truly build a healthy life and partnership with. I was lucky enough to get everything I wanted and am still immensely grateful for that every day.

We knew fairly quickly that we had something special, and it was time to fold in the most important ingredients of our individual lives: our kids. After we'd been together for a few weeks, Jeannette met my kids before I met hers, and for them, it wasn't a big deal. I had already been divorced for a couple of years and separated long before that. I had also previously dated two people, and so my kids had met them and had distant, superficial relationships with them. When I described Jeannette to them, they were excited to meet her.

Jeannette

I met Paul's kids for the first time when he was moving from his house in the mountains to an apartment close to where I lived. I went over to his house to help them with packing, and then we had a game night. It all went really well. I felt an instant bond form with Mariah on that first night. She was friendly and interactive and seemed to appreciate my help and attention. Ashley was older and had a more complicated relationship with her mother, so she was understandably a bit more cautious. She was kind and polite but obviously distant.

When I felt comfortable, we decided it was time for Paul and his family to meet my kids. We all went on a very interesting bowling excursion. My oldest son, Christian, and his girlfriend (who is now his wife) were there, as were Anthony and Danie. At this point, Christian was already eighteen, Anthony was fifteen, and Danie was ten. Paul's girls, who were sixteen and eleven,

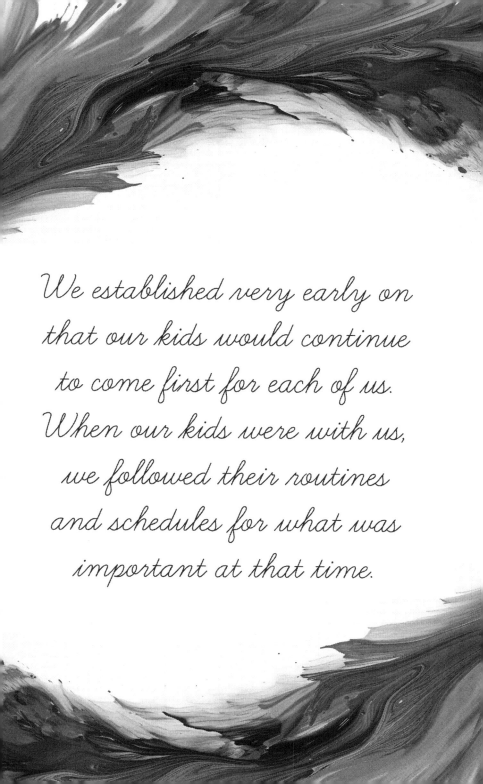

We established very early on
that our kids would continue
to come first for each of us.
When our kids were with us,
we followed their routines
and schedules for what was
important at that time.

came with him. To say this was an awkward situation would be a massive understatement. My kids sat together on one side, and Paul's kids sat on the opposite side. They all avoided conversation and eye contact. My kids were more apprehensive than Mariah and Ashley because, again, my ex-husband and I hadn't fought during my first marriage, so our divorce had been a tremendous shock to them. They truly hadn't had enough time to digest it all. Looking back, I should have waited longer to give them more time to adjust.

Danie, my youngest, was ten at the time. She was the most visibly skeptical of Paul and his kids. She sat at the edge of the bowling semicircle, disgruntled and staring angrily off into the distance. She must have been glancing over at us occasionally because, at one point, Paul touched my back. She gave new meaning to the phrase *If looks could kill* at that moment.

Later in the relationship, we participated in a class about stepfamilies called *The Smart Stepfamily* based on the book by speaker and therapist, Ron Deal. We really connected with a great metaphor that was shared, comparing a stepfamily to a delicious dinner being prepared in a crock pot. In the pot, there is the roast, some carrots, the other vegetables, and the potatoes. Each ingredient adds its own unique and special flavor. The carrots are the hardest vegetable, and therefore, take the longest to cook. It took Danie a long time to come around, but she eventually warmed up and became tender, more generously adding her individual flavor to our family. Danie was our carrot.

Paul and I had met in August, introduced our kids to each other in the fall, and by December, he was ready to propose. I told him it was way too soon. I was sure my kids weren't ready for that. Although I had started to care deeply for him and his girls, I was not so sure I was ready for another marriage. "What-ifs" started flooding my mind. What if this was all happening too fast? What if Paul wasn't who he seemed to be? What if I agreed to marry him and things changed for the worse after the wedding? The only thing I felt 100% confident about was that I didn't want to fall into the same cycle my mother had been in when we were growing up.

Each of my kids reacted to Paul differently. Anthony warmed up to Paul quickly, but it took some time for Christian, who was older. Of course, we knew Danie was the toughest. Paul was the first man I had agreed to meet even though there were several that I had been talking to on *Match*. This was all new for my kids. It had been a very scary thing for me to meet anyone because I had kids. I was especially protective of my young daughter; I had grown up around men my mother dated.

It was comforting and reassuring that Paul had two girls, and it was so apparent that his girls loved him. He was a fun dad. He loved spending time with them, and I just loved the relationship that they had. It was much different than anything I had ever experienced as a child. We established very early on that our kids would continue to come first for each of us. When our kids were with us, we followed their routines and schedules for what was important at that time. For example, he would come over for dinner and bring Mariah and Ashley, and they would always leave in time for their established bedtime. Even though the relationships were evolving, we wanted to provide them with as much stability as we possibly could.

While we were dating, we focused on helping our kids feel comfortable and loved, but also were intentional about carving out some quality alone time. Christian was in college and Anthony and Danie were with me except when they went to their dad's on Wednesdays and every other weekend. Ashley never went to see her mom, but Mariah did. Paul eventually allowed Ashley to spend some time with her mom, and that gave us more time without the kids. It was so incredibly important to cherish that time and use it well. When you already have children, it's hard to find time alone as a couple and to really be able to continue to learn about each other. We were very intentional about spending time together with the kids and without the kids.

Paul traveled for work, as he still does today, but he's always been very good about making plans for us to be together when he is home. This has allowed our relationship to flourish.

> " I wanted to believe him, but I needed to know that he had been 100% honest with me about everything. "

Paul proposed on April 20th, eight months after we had met, and I felt ready, but still slightly apprehensive. Although he'd given me no reason to doubt him, I was still scarred from having my trust shattered so many times in my previous marriage. Early in our relationship when Paul had shared his story of addiction and recovery with me, he told me that he had taken a polygraph for his ex-wife to prove to her that he was truthful. He'd even shared those results with me at that time. Now, faced with the prospect of entering another marriage, I asked him to take one for me. Things were moving very quickly, and I knew I loved him, but I needed reassurance that everything he told me was true. He had told me once that all addicts are expert liars, and he was a recovering addict. I wanted to believe him, but I needed to know that he had been 100% honest with me about everything. It was the security I needed to move forward with him.

He immediately agreed to the polygraph and passed every part of it. The concept of having a significant other take a polygraph to prove their honesty may seem extreme, but as a victim of abuse and deceit, it was what I needed at the time. When I have mentored women, I share this with them. The polygraph is a tool to build trust when it has been badly broken. When you have been repeatedly lied to or cheated on, you need a place to start. Paul's willingness to take the test and his passing results gave me that reassurance and starting point that I needed. It also helped me regain some confidence in my own judgement and instincts. After seeing those results, I was able to say yes confidently and joyfully to his proposal.

We decided upon a small October wedding. Anthony was happy for me. He wanted me to be happy. Christian was already on his own; I didn't think it would affect him as much as the others at that time. Danie was clearly not happy and resorted to the silent treatment. Again, had we given it more time, the reactions to our big news may have been different. Paul remembers his girls being happy for him upon hearing the news.

We did not live together until just before we married. We initially thought about living in my house, but it would have been too small. In retrospect, it probably was wise for us all to start fresh in a new home. So, we bought a house and all moved in together about a week before the wedding. Paul and I stayed in separate rooms. I had stopped sleeping in the same bed with my ex several years earlier, so Danie had grown used to sharing a bed with me. As the wedding day approached, she asked where Paul was going to sleep after the wedding. I said, "Well, I'm going to sleep in the same room as Paul, and you'll have your whole room to yourself." That seemed to provide a bit of consolation, but I could tell her wheels were turning, and not in a positive way. She wasn't sold on the addition of Paul's girls to our family either. She was especially annoyed by Mariah. The two of them didn't interact at all when we all moved in together and for quite some time afterward. We both vividly recall them encountering each other at breakfast or in the hallways of the new house in awkward silence.

The other kids seemed to handle the move a bit better. Christian was in college and living on campus, so the move didn't impact him as much. Ashley was a senior and the oldest living at home. She was busy with her own life, going to school and playing basketball. Anthony was Sophomore and was busy with school, working, wrestling and also had a girlfriend.

I (Jeannette) was very excited to be married to Paul, but to say I wasn't nervous would be a lie. The situation with Danie and Mariah was tough for me. I am at my best when things are going smoothly, and I don't enjoy walking on eggshells. I knew I couldn't force the girls to like each other, and that I had to let them adjust to our new family dynamics at their own pace. Knowing it was the right thing to do was easy; doing it was extremely difficult for me.

Paul was just excited to be married. Since he traveled for work quite a bit, he wasn't exposed to the drama between Danie and Mariah as much. His focus was on getting married, and he figured everything else would fall into place.

Since it was the second one for both of us, our wedding was low-key and low-budget. We had decided together that we just wanted a small wedding with family and close friends. We had a guest list of around seventy people. My uncle was our photographer. Our wedding party was made up of our kids, and we saw that as beautifully symbolic of us all becoming one family unit. My boys walked me down the aisle, a now-cherished memory. We had a small reception and just served cake and coffee. Paul was excited to leave as soon as we could. I can still hear him eagerly telling me, "Let's cut the cake so we can go!" He wanted us to be able to celebrate our marriage and officially start our journey together away from others and from all the distractions.

After the wedding, my mom stayed with the kids, and we went to Vail for three days. It was a short but wonderful trip. Paul's employer at the time generously paid for everything, which was pretty amazing. In January, we were able to travel to Thailand and Singapore and enjoy an incredible, worry-free honeymoon.

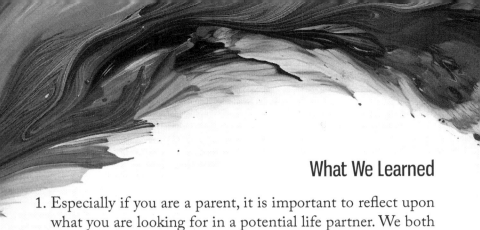

What We Learned

1. Especially if you are a parent, it is important to reflect upon what you are looking for in a potential life partner. We both made lists of characteristics and thought about non-negotiables as well. Neither of us was willing to enter another unhealthy relationship.

2. Just as it should be at the top of the list for yourself, prioritize emotional health when considering potential partners.

3. Consider the time your kids might need to adjust to the ideas of you dating, entering into a relationship, and ultimately re-marrying. Don't rush through any of these stages when kids are involved.

4. Honor family routines and practices even as your families begin to co-exist. Chances are your kids are dealing with many changes and emotions when you begin a new relationship, so minimize unnecessary changes to rules and routines.

5. As you begin to spend time together as families, be sure to also carve out time as a couple to continue to strengthen your relationship.

four

Beginning to Blend

"The most important ingredient we put into any relationship is not what we say or what we do, but what we are."
– Stephen Covey

The successful blending of ingredients in any recipe requires precision, care, and patience. When blending families, all of these things, plus a huge helping of authenticity, are crucial. Our kids all adapted to our new family dynamic in their own ways and in their own time.

Of my three kids (Jeannette), Anthony connected with Paul quickly and seemed to adjust well to having Paul around. His relationship with his dad was strained while he was growing up, which may have made it easier for him to connect with Paul without guilt. He was a rebellious and disrespectful teenager and young adult—really up into his twenties. Paul remained patient and supportive through it all. He proved that he wasn't going anywhere regardless of how difficult Anthony could be.

Paul was always there to support him and gained his respect by attending all of his sporting events. One of the great things about this was that it was obvious that Paul enjoyed doing this.

He was being himself, not doing it because he felt he had to. That patience and authenticity helped Anthony to gain trust and a high level of respect for Paul. Paul is also often more logical than emotional, and sometimes that is what Anthony needs. There are things that Anthony has gone to Paul with that he hasn't even shared with me. For example, he has shared with Paul some of his experiences from being deployed to Afghanistan when he was in the Marine Corps. That's the type of relationship they have. Anthony doesn't hesitate to ask Paul's opinion or advice when needed. I think he is comfortable with him, and he knows Paul loves him. He has matured in the last several years, and he owns up to all of the things he did as a child and teenager. We've both been able to rest a bit easier at night knowing that he has gotten over the hump of making bad decisions. He is now married with a great job and a home of his own. He will still call Paul for advice when he has a big decision to make. When we told him we were writing this book, he wanted to be quoted, "Paul is the best stepdad a guy could ask for!"

Paul wasn't the only new relationship in his life, however. He and Ashley butted heads a few times. Again, Anthony could be disrespectful, especially as a teenager. One thing Ashley had learned from her mom was respect; so, she didn't like the way Anthony spoke to me. They had a few big fights about this while we were adjusting to our new lives together.

Christian was eighteen when Paul came along, and initially, he didn't have a close relationship with him. He wasn't around him as much as the other kids. Because he was older, he was really busy establishing a life of his own. It took time for him to develop trust and a relationship with Paul. Christian is one to sit back and watch. I think he observed Paul and his relationships with Danie, Anthony, and myself, and this helped him to gain his own understanding of who Paul was. Today, they have a great relationship. He clearly respects Paul, and there isn't anything he wouldn't come to Paul with.

I (Jeannette) recall praying that I would love Paul's girls like they were my own. Although that did not happen overnight, it did happen. For me, building a relationship with Mariah was easy. I focused on letting her get to know me without pushing myself on her. Since Mariah's relationship with her biological mom was not the greatest, I tried to be there and support her in any way that I could. I focused on doing the motherly things that her mom wasn't doing. I went to as many of her school events as possible, took an interest in the things that seemed to matter to her, and tried to spend quality, conflict-free time with her. I was determined to be a role model that both girls could respect and emulate. I hoped they would notice, appreciate, and remember not only the way I treated them, but also how I treated their father.

Of all the kids, Danie and Ashley were the ones that we needed to patiently peel layers back by slowly and consistently creating bonds with them. Danie was very angry and cold towards me (Paul) for about two years. I would walk into the room, and she would not even speak to me. I'm pretty sure that if I would have died during that time, she would not have shed a tear or attended the funeral.

I bought Jeannette a keychain at one point that had *"I heart Paul"* written on it. Danie would secretly bite it just to show how much she disagreed with that message. It took about five years for her to gradually warm up to me. Consistency was key with her. I had to be even-tempered and consistent, which I could do because of the work I had done in therapy. This wasn't easy; in fact, I had to actively decide every day to love her even if she didn't love me. I knew she was finally warming up to me when she started asking Jeannette when I would be home to help her with her homework instead of just having her mom help her.

Building those relationships with stepchildren takes time, and it's important to remember that they haven't known you all of their lives. Their relationships with their biological parents likely shape how they approach building a relationship with you as the new stepparent. Jeannette's ex-husband also had a relationship with the kids, so that played into how Danie connected with me (Paul). Danie may have had a bit of an internal struggle going on that made her feel as though if she loved me, she would be betraying her dad. In a way, Jeannette's situation was almost easier because my kids didn't have a good role model for a mother. I just had to stand my ground with Danie and make sure she knew that I wasn't going anywhere; I was always going to be there for her. It was unconditional. Building that sort of trust takes time. It took six years to build the level of trust that allowed her to fully love and respect me. Today, I'm as close to Danie as I am to Ashley and Mariah. I was honored to be able to give a speech at her wedding. I purchased her a new, wooden *I Heart Paul* keychain and shared the story behind it.

Ashley also had a hard time adjusting to our families coming together. Paul and his ex had been separated for quite some time, and she had become accustomed to staying by herself when Paul traveled for work. Paul would check up on her and neighbors would keep an eye on things, but she was pretty much functioning on her own. When we came together, she suddenly had a new family bombarding her, and she had some new rules and routines to adjust to. For one thing, there were more people to share with. She suddenly had to share the car, the television, and other things that she was used to having to herself. She also had to be more accountable for communicating her plans and whereabouts. She was a great kid, and it wasn't that I (Jeannette) ever thought she was out doing things she shouldn't be doing. It was more about respect, especially since I was the parent in charge when Paul was traveling. I was juggling the many responsibilities that come with running a household. Among those responsibilities was the coordination of schedules and family dinners, so it was important for me to know where everyone was. I also tended to worry if I didn't know where any of the kids were, so I insisted that they check in frequently and let me know if plans changed. It was a tough transition for her. At the onset of our relationship, she was very disconnected from everything—an angry child. It was clear that she was dealing with a lot of trauma, and as a result, she was extremely unhappy. I was very conscientious about not trying or pushing too hard with her. We gradually started to spend a lot of time together, and I tried to share who I was with her. I understood that she needed time and space. She needed someone to take a genuine interest in who she was, but it had to be at her pace. Eventually, our conversations became more meaningful, and we started to do fun things together, like shopping for her prom dress.

No matter how old stepchildren are, you have to meet them where they are and show them respect.

Many times, stepparents think the kids have to like them, but I (Jeannette) was painfully aware that no rule said they had to like me as a stepmother or at all, for that matter. I was coming into their family just like they were coming into mine. No matter how old stepchildren are, you have to meet them where they are and show them respect. Now, Ashley and I have an authentically beautiful relationship. Just this year, on Mother's Day, I was texting her and telling her how proud I am of her for being such a great mom. She said, "Well, you know you are the reason; you're the one that showed me how to be a mom." This still brings tears to my eyes when I think about it. It's been truly rewarding and so special.

For me (Paul), Jeannette's ability to accept and love my kids even when it was difficult made me love her even more deeply. Ashley was difficult; she didn't just have a shell to come out of; she had built up a cement wall. Jeannette was steadfast and patient with her, and for that, I am still so grateful. She helped break down that wall in ways that I would never have been able to. Building in time for conversations and connections around everything from friends to boys, to Ashley's evolving style, I vividly remember watching the relationship grow and flourish. Ashley has matured a great deal, especially since getting married and having kids of her own. Her relationship with Jeannette has also continued to grow. She and her husband, Rob, bought a house, and Ashley admittedly doesn't have a decorating bone in her body. Jeannette was invited to Alaska to help decorate their house. It was great because they both have great jobs and had a budget for decorating, so Jeannette was like, "Heck yeah, I'll spend your decorating budget!" To me, it meant so much and just affirmed that we are one big family that truly loves and supports each other.

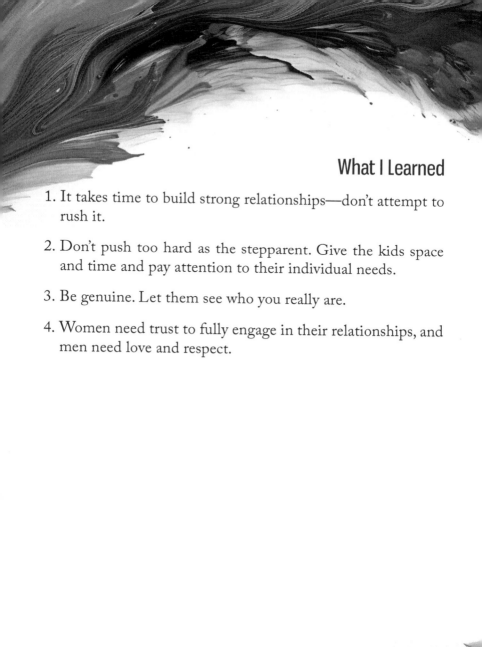

What I Learned

1. It takes time to build strong relationships—don't attempt to rush it.

2. Don't push too hard as the stepparent. Give the kids space and time and pay attention to their individual needs.

3. Be genuine. Let them see who you really are.

4. Women need trust to fully engage in their relationships, and men need love and respect.

Part Two

Flavor Detractors

five

The Ex Factor

"Forgiveness is not an occasional act, it is a constant attitude."
- Martin Luther King Jr.

Jeannette

Since the divorce, my relationship with my ex has continuously evolved. Initially, I did have to put boundaries in place. When we would talk on the phone, he would want to talk about me or us. I think he thought there was a chance of us getting back together until Paul and I got married. At one point, he told me that although we were not together, he would always love me. I had to remind him often that our conversations needed to remain focused only on our kids.

There was a time that he was very manipulative, especially just after Paul and I started dating. He would mainly try to manipulate my time. When he was supposed to have Danie and Anthony, he would have things come up abruptly and say that he couldn't take them. It felt like he hoped to interfere with my plans. Finally, I said, "Listen, you know the schedule, you know when you're supposed to have them, and you need to plan around that. Yes, if there's an emergency or something like that, I always want to be the first one that you come to. Unless it's an emergency, you should never have to reschedule the time that you have your kids because it's set in stone, and it's invaluable." We were able to gradually work through that and honor the schedules we had created. Our typical schedule was for him to have the kids every other weekend and then Wednesday nights after school overnight. He would take them to school, and then I would pick them up on Thursdays after school. After I set the boundaries and clearly communicated my expectations, this worked well.

> **"**
> *I did my best to never speak negatively about my ex-husband around the kids and to respect him and the time that he had with them.* **"**

While reflecting upon how to manage my evolving relationship with my ex, I recalled doing daycare when my kids were young. There was a divorced couple that had a great working relationship when it came to their kids. I wanted that, too, and vowed to never use my kids as pawns or make them feel they were in the middle. I did my best to never speak negatively about my ex-husband around the kids and to respect him and the time that he had with them. We also worked hard to communicate directly with each other rather than trying to communicate through the kids. We didn't fight. It was like we co-owned a business (our kids) and that was where our focus needed to be. Establishing those boundaries up-front would have saved me some major frustration, but it was something I was learning how to do through experience and therapy.

As previously mentioned, our divorce was probably hardest on my youngest, Danie. She was very protective of my ex after Paul and I met because she knew he was alone. I think in some ways, this made it harder for her to like Paul. My ex was not great at spending time with her while we were married. She was very much a mama's girl and didn't always want her dad. During the separation and divorce, she had to rely on her dad when she was with him. It was a good thing for their relationship. Our divorce forced him into being a dad and spending more quality time with her. They now have a strong relationship as a result. She isn't afraid to be honest with him and confront him when needed. She will speak her mind, he will listen, consider her perspective, and respond. I'm not sure they would have had that kind of relationship if we hadn't gotten divorced.

Splitting the time between the two households got harder for Danie as she grew older. When she became a junior in high school, like most teens, she was gaining independence and becoming more involved in sports and her social life. Life became busier for her, and it became a real hassle to pack up and take her things over to her dad's house for overnights. As a result, she started to stay with him less. She would still go over and maybe spend the day with him but didn't end up staying for the night as often. Looking back, I think my ex and I handled that very well. He didn't harass her about not staying over, and I didn't tell her she had to. We let her make those decisions. She didn't ask for us to get divorced; none of our kids did, so we worked to do what we had to do to make it the best possible situation for them. None of us wanted any of our kids to be burdened by the choices that we had made.

After Danie graduated from high school and began preparing to go to college, my ex suddenly announced that he was moving to Wyoming for a couple of years. That's where he's from, and his family is there. He has been there ever since, but still occasionally will come back and see the kids for important occasions.

My relationship with him today is cordial. We've learned to get along and come to terms with the fact that when you have kids with someone, that person is going to be in your life forever. We've been able to come together for important life events like birthdays, graduations, and funerals. In fact, Danie graduated from a nursing program recently, and he came back to celebrate with us. We were all able to go out to dinner together comfortably and focus on celebrating her accomplishment.

My ex is personable; he's always kind and friendly when people meet him. He just didn't know how to be a husband because he came from a very dysfunctional upbringing. We all learn by example, from how our fathers treated our mothers, or vice versa. I don't have any hard feelings or animosity towards him at all. Like me, he has many wounds and a lot of baggage from growing up that make him who he is. I now recognize that, emotionally, he stuffs everything deep down inside himself. In twenty years of marriage, I saw him cry only twice. There's so much trauma and pain in him that he has carried around with him throughout his life.

I'm sure if my ex would have talked with Danie and let her know that it was okay to like Paul, it would have helped Danie tremendously. I believe there was a part of her that did not want to betray her dad by liking Paul. I don't think he ever spoke ill of Paul but, rather, didn't say much. If he'd given her permission to like him, things may have improved a bit more quickly than they did. Of course, it would be difficult to approve of the significant other of an ex-spouse if you weren't confident the person was good. Typically, though, you know who your ex-spouse is, and hopefully, that he or she is not likely to marry someone that would cause harm to your children.

Danie has told me that she has friends with divorced parents who have had a horrible experience because their parents didn't get along at all. She has shared that, in her opinion, my ex and I did a really good job of making a bad situation the best it could have been for our kids. That was the goal, and I do think we've succeeded in that. The kids have the best of both worlds because they have the love and support of their dad and Paul.

As for me, my marriage now is the complete opposite of my first marriage; I finally have what I dreamed about all of those years ago as a young girl. This is without a doubt because Paul and I both did the hard work we needed to do on and for ourselves before coming together. This is something my ex and I obviously never did, and the impact on our marriage was fatal.

Paul

Jeannette is so correct about the importance of setting boundaries with the ex-spouse right away. I should have set more boundaries sooner with my ex. Until I did, she went out of her way to create chaos and drama. Once, while I was traveling and she had Mariah, she and Mariah got into a fight. Hysterical, she contacted me, and I was immediately concerned for Mariah's safety. I asked Jeannette to go and pick her up. She had to leave Anthony's senior wrestling banquet to go meet the sheriff at my ex's house. Mariah ended up being okay and decided to stay with her mother, which was a relief, but Jeannette had been robbed of the opportunity to celebrate Anthony's wrestling success with him because of her antics. Another time, she called Jeannette in a drunken stupor to badmouth me. After that episode, we both agreed that enough was enough, and Jeannette urged me to set some clear boundaries with her. I sent her an email informing her that we weren't going to tolerate her erratic behavior any longer. I explained that she needed to communicate respectfully through me, not Jeannette. I was clear that if she couldn't do that, we would be getting law enforcement involved. It did work, and it was something that should have been done with her much earlier.

> **"**
> *When you are engulfed in the emotions and drama of divorce and the aftermath, it can be hard to envision parenting separately or on your own.*
> **"**

There is no doubt in my mind that divorce made me a better parent. I evolved even more as a parent after getting custody of my girls. My relationships with my girls would not be what they are today had I not gotten divorced. When you are engulfed in the emotions and drama of divorce and the aftermath, it can be hard to envision parenting separately or on your own. It is 100% a choice. Some parents feel that they can't live up to being a good parent, so they just abandon their children like my ex-wife did. So many guys think, *If I can't be married, I'll just leave and free myself of all of the responsibilities of being a husband and a father.* Then, if there is a remarriage, the stepparent really needs to step up and be a good parent. Luckily, Jeannette was willing to do that for my girls, and her ex didn't abandon his kids.

I've gotten along fine with Jeannette's ex-husband, and we eventually all transitioned well. Thinking back to the friends who were vocal about their disapproval of our marriage, I know they once told someone they were praying that Jeannette and her ex would get back together, even after we married. I do have to wonder how they may have influenced him and how he handled things with Danie at the beginning of our marriage. He had to have known that she was not too fond of me, and as previously mentioned, likely didn't do much to help her learn to accept me.

When Jeannette's ex stopped seeing the kids as much and eventually moved to Wyoming, I felt more responsibility as a stepparent. In retrospect, this was a good thing, because it allowed me to grow closer to them. I felt I had more time with them and the freedom to develop strong relationships without stepping on their dad's toes.

It can be strange when you are blending families because in our case, Jeannette's kids went with their dad every other weekend and on Wednesdays, and I was with them the rest of the time. I physically stepped into the role of parent to them when we started living together because I was with them more than their father was. That's tough for some stepfamilies because of that partial shift. It is a physical shift in time spent together, but not necessarily an automatic or complete shift in the connections.

If you are the one coming into the relationship and household, and you aren't ready for that responsibility or role, things can get tricky. A lot of stepparents get into a relationship and fall in love. Then they meet the kids. As they get more involved with the kids, relationships may grow, but then they go home to their own environments. Even if the relationships are developing, the reality doesn't hit home until the families come together to live. Then the kids are there all the time, and that can be a big transition, not only for the kids, but also for the stepparent. It is essential to be sure you are ready for that transition before bringing two families together.

It is also important to honor the fact that the involved children have another parent. Regardless of the mental health or stability of that parent, there is another parent connected to your stepchild(ren). You are unlikely to take the place of that biological parent. In our case, Jeannette has, but it's been over time. A lot of stepparents want to come in and take over for that missing parent immediately, and that doesn't happen overnight. It takes time. Trying to force it often breeds rebellion and resentment.

Finally, it is important to avoid speaking negatively about your ex in front of the kids

Finally, it is important to avoid speaking negatively about your ex in front of the kids. This can definitely harm relationships and come back to haunt you. It also often, even if unintentionally, puts kids in the middle, causing them even more stress and trauma. Never forget the fact that this person, regardless of his or her mistakes, is Mom or Dad to them. You may be wondering how we can give this advice while also sharing the struggles we've had with our ex-spouses. All our children are aware of the stories we share throughout this book. Through their involvement in much of the drama we've described, and our honesty in addressing questions they have had along the way, they've learned the details of each of our failed marriages. However, we have been careful not to disparage our exes or do anything to intentionally tarnish their relationships with them. As adults, we are confident that they can combine all their knowledge and experiences from the past to form their own opinions and pursue relationships with our exes however they see fit.

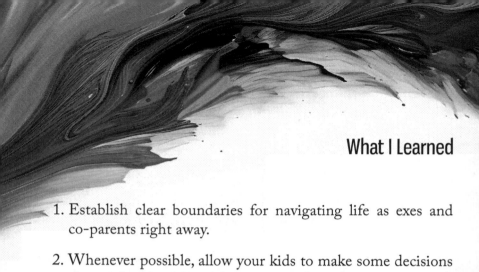

What I Learned

1. Establish clear boundaries for navigating life as exes and co-parents right away.

2. Whenever possible, allow your kids to make some decisions about where and how they are spending their time in each household.

3. Help your kids to understand that your ex deserves love and happiness. Give them permission to accept, and yes, even like or love your ex's new partner.

4. Before committing to marriage, be sure you are prepared to physically step into the role of parent with the children of your significant other.

5. As the stepparent, give it time with the kids. Do not try to replace their biological parent.

6. Never bash your ex in front of your kids.

Part Three

Tweaking the Recipe

Six

What We Did Right and What We Did Wrong

*"We do not learn from experience. We learn
from reflecting on experience."*
– John Dewey

Mastering any recipe requires patience, flexibility, and a willingness to learn from your mistakes to perfect it and make it your own. Blending families is no different, especially if the chefs have little experience. As much as humanly possible, it is important to discuss finances, parenting styles, schedules, and how you will carve out sacred, quality time for each other before blending families. Shifting the mindset of *what and who is mine versus yours* to *it's ALL ours* is also crucial. Traditional marriage is designed to give you time to figure all of this out together as a couple before bringing children into the mix. Blending families doesn't allow you that luxury; you are all in from the start, so having a solid recipe for success is crucial.

Money

Jeannette

When blending families, you are also blending income and debt. It is crucial to have a plan for how you will handle finances as a couple prior to marriage. This is something we did not do well. Designations of who would manage our money and pay the bills were addressed as they came up for us. Luckily, it worked out okay for us, but it could have been a really big issue in our relationship because Paul was more of the breadwinner in the relationship. If we had kept accounts separate, he could have done a lot of fun things with his kids that I would not have had the money to do with mine. We had to decide that we were truly a team. There can be no "we" if the money is separated. Within a week of our marriage, everything became joint even though we hadn't discussed this in advance.

The money issue was still really difficult for me for quite some time. Because of my past, I was afraid to spend any money. In my previous marriage, we didn't have a lot of money, and everything was allocated. There was never anything extra left over. I also didn't feel like the money in my new marriage was our money at first; I felt like it was Paul's. Even though I worked, and my money went into joint checking and savings accounts, I just felt weird spending the money. I remember Paul actually needing to say, "If you need gas, get gas. If you need groceries, get groceries." I was still very cautious about what I spent. Old habits are hard to break. Things were also a bit tight at times. Eventually, Christian transferred to a different school and moved back home. So, we had all five kids home at one time, and groceries for that many people got expensive. I was very cautious about what I spent back then. Now, not so much.

Early in our marriage, I remember we had a conflict around money. Paul made a statement insinuating that he was using his money for something that had come up with one of my kids. I had to stop him. I told him that he wasn't going to speak to me that way and that we needed to act as a partnership. I told him that I didn't need him. I wanted him, but I didn't need him. I told him that his helping to pay for the situation was not him *having one over on me* because I would have taken care of it no matter what. He was shocked and speechless for a moment. I was using my newly-found voice to communicate that yes, I could be sweet, but I was no longer afraid to stand up and express how I was feeling. I was going to clearly communicate what I needed and what was and wasn't okay. That is what therapy had done for me. After he got over his shock, I think it made sense to him, and he understood where I was coming from. It has never happened again. The bottom line is separating resources or tracking how they are allocated based on biological family lines can be quite damaging.

> " Money is a very big issue in relationships and can be an even bigger one when blending families, so you really have to let go and realize the money is shared no matter what. "

Luckily, aside from that one incident, Paul has never been one to approach money as his and mine. He never made it an issue when the kids needed something. Child support didn't come close to covering all of the financial needs that came with raising our children. He was always very willing to make sure they had everything they needed. Occasionally, if something big would come up, he might suggest that my ex-husband help cover some of those costs. That was fair. Money is a very big issue in relationships and can be an even bigger one when blending families, so you really have to let go and realize the money is shared no matter what.

Paul

It's true that, just as it can be in any relationship, money can become a real issue in a blended family. Our relationship was tested a few times with issues revolving around finances. Just before Anthony graduated high school, he got into some legal trouble. As a stepparent, you can do one of two things: say he's not my kid or say he's not my biological kid, but he does need to be treated as my own. Some stepparents might say, "He's on his own;" "Have his dad pay for it;" or "That's not my kid; he's yours." We had to get an attorney for him. As a stepparent, you have to be willing to assume the role of parent and give unconditional love, even if and when there is another parent in the picture. That's what I chose to do in that situation.

Another issue related to finances that we should have discussed in advance was how we were going to support the kids as they worked toward independence. Christian had already started college, so we weren't paying for that. When Ashley went to school, we paid for a good majority of her college. Anthony went to a culinary school, but he was also in the Marines, so his tuition was covered. When Danie and Mariah went to school, we paid for it just as we had handled Ashley's college expenses. So Christian really did get the raw end of the deal when it came to school. We didn't discuss how we were going to handle those kinds of things ahead of time, so it has occasionally come up with Christian. Had we communicated a clear plan to equitably support all of them, we could have alleviated his feelings of not being as strongly supported as the others.

Workshops and Therapy

As previously mentioned, we each benefitted from the life-changing impact of therapy before we came together as a couple. We also did premarital counseling, which was highly beneficial. I (Paul) consider my therapist to be one of the best therapists in the United States. He's that good. He's been my counselor for twenty years, and I now consider him a close friend as well.

One of the great things about him is that he speaks *woman*. Early on, I could tell him something confusing that Jeannette had said or asked for, and he was able to help me understand what she meant or needed. He just understands the differences between how women and men think and behave, and having that perspective has been so helpful.

Almost all of our children, with the exception of Christian, have had some amount of individual therapy, but we never did therapy as a family, and that was a mistake. Each person in our blended family brings unique strands of experiences and trauma. Learning how to navigate the challenges that arise because of this along with all of the everyday challenges that come with blending families would likely be a game-changer.

Can you figure it all out on your own? Possibly. But that can take precious time and potentially cause more trauma and wounding. We wish we had taken advantage of existing workshops on stepfamilies; working through challenges together with an expert would have likely saved us all some heartache and helped us capitalize on the time we had to create and strengthen family bonds. We would strongly recommend family therapy to anyone considering a second marriage that incorporates stepchildren.

Discipline

Discipline was another thing we failed to discuss before getting married. When it came to discipline, we each naturally handled our own kids. If Paul had an issue with my kids, we would talk about how to handle it and vice versa. He traveled extensively for work. So, if he was gone, and I had the girls, I could correct them when necessary. Luckily, they didn't need a lot of discipline. Neither of us directly disciplined our step kids without discussing the issue and plan with each other first. We didn't feel comfortable doing that. We also were cognizant of the fact that we did not want any of the kids to feel like we were trying to come in and replace their other parent.

We recognized early on that we had different parenting styles. Paul can sometimes be stern, harsh, and loud. I (Jeannette) knew my kids would not be responsive to that. I also sensed that I might become defensive if I witnessed him disciplining them in that way. This likely would have caused more difficulties than it would have been worth within all of our relationships. But I needed to communicate this to him in a way that didn't cause *him* to become frustrated or defensive. With time and experience, we both became more reflective about how to communicate with each other when it came to issues with the kids. We learned the necessity of remembering that we are on the same team and of actively listening to each other with open minds. Sometimes that natural urge to become defensive can be extremely strong, and it can take everything you've got to resist it, but resisting it only strengthens the team. There is also value in taking some time to think about the best time and way to respond when things do get heated. We've learned that timing, delivery, and word choice really do matter when working through parenting issues as a couple.

Certainly, if anything drastic occurred, we made decisions together. I (Jeannette) would also be sure to communicate with my ex-husband about anything major that happened with our kids. We really were just figuring it out as we went, which usually worked out okay, but probably would have been less stressful for all involved had we gone into it with more of a plan.

Respect

We were strongly committed to modeling and cultivating respect, and in turn, eventually earned it from all of our kids. When you are bringing families together, kids can try to test boundaries and come between you as a couple. Danie definitely tried to do this at the beginning of our marriage. She would disagree with Paul about something, come to me about it, and then get angry when I didn't take her side. She asked me once why I always stood up for him. I told her there were three good reasons. He was my

We wish we had taken advantage of existing workshops on stepfamilies; working through challenges together with an expert would have likely saved us all some heartache and helped us capitalize on the time we had to create and strengthen family bonds.

husband, he was right, and if he hadn't been right, I would have told him that. I explained to her that she did not have to like him, but she absolutely had to treat him with respect.

> *The stepparent needs to respect the stepchildren and where they are developmentally and emotionally to successfully gain respect from them.*

The fact that we were bringing children with a large range of ages together taught us so much. It is important to understand that different kids are going to react and adjust differently to divorce and the blending of a new family. Some younger children might just go with the flow and occasionally react emotionally. Kids who are between ten and fifteen are more likely to act and react more emotionally. Those who are older may seem to develop negative and disrespectful attitudes. How a stepparent responds to that is extremely important. If he/she tries to stomp that attitude down or put the stepchild in his or her place, it often backfires and causes rebellion. The stepparent needs to respect the stepchildren and where they are developmentally and emotionally to successfully gain respect from them.

Providing Support Regardless of Age

Divorce and remarriage absolutely impacts older kids. Don't make the false assumption that they are not affected as intensely as the younger kids. Our son, Christian, was the oldest when our relationship began. We may have made some incorrect assumptions that he was fine throughout our blending process. I took Danie and Anthony to therapy but assumed that, because he was older, Christian didn't need it. That was likely one of my incorrect assumptions.

When he was growing up, Christian was very much a mama's boy. He was very loving, just like a big teddy bear. The picture of emotional stability, he's always been a rule follower. I recall when he transferred colleges and moved home, after we'd been married a short time, he had this attitude. It was so different from how he had been when he was a child. He was never rude or disrespectful to Paul, but often took his anger and frustration out on me. I wondered what was going on with him. He seemed like a different person. Upon further reflection, I finally realized that this was the first time that he lived in a home where his parents weren't together. I was with somebody else, and he was plopped into this new family situation. Ashley's experience was similar. She was forced into a completely different family dynamic just as she was learning to be more independent.

> **"**
> *Patience, compassion, and grace are necessary as they process the strong, and understandably painful, confusing emotions that come with divorce-induced change.* **"**

Just because older kids have to adjust differently doesn't mean they aren't adjusting, and although the support they need might look different, they still absolutely need it. Patience, compassion, and grace are necessary as they process the strong, and understandably painful, confusing emotions that come with divorce-induced change.

We've heard many stories about people divorcing when their kids are in their twenties or even their thirties. They think their kids are adults with their own lives, so the stepfamily situation is no big deal. But when they come home, and the family dynamic is completely different, it is a big deal. Oftentimes, they end up not blending because everything is so different, and they are already out of the house. There is no impetus for them to blend. Then, when family functions occur, interactions can range from uncomfortable to disastrous. Remember, even when we are older, some of us might still be stuck at age twelve emotionally.

Older children in this situation might really be deeply feeling the absence of the other biological parent. They might also feel protective of that parent, and/or resentful of the stepparent that is there in his or her place. Since they are older and likely busy with their own lives, they might also see no reason to bond with

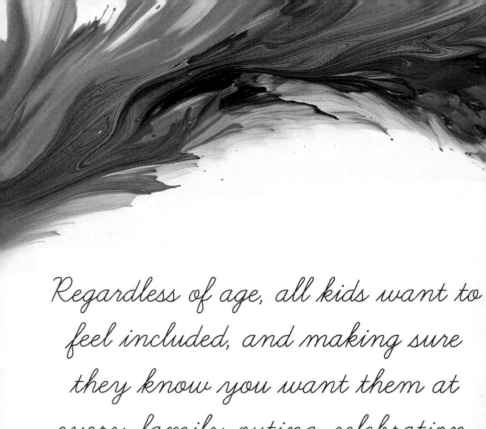

Regardless of age, all kids want to feel included, and making sure they know you want them at every family outing, celebration, and trip helps them feel like they are truly an important part of the family structure.

the stepparent or stepsiblings. Helping them understand their role as an important ingredient in the blended family is crucial.

Regardless of age, all kids want to feel included, and making sure they know you want them at every family outing, celebration, and trip helps them feel like they are truly an important part of the family structure. When they are older, it's helpful to have family gatherings that are light and create a space for them to interact. We've found playing games to be a great way to provide a relaxed atmosphere where older kids can get to know each other.

Equity

Throughout our lives together, we've tried to prioritize treating all of the kids equally. When they were in school, we worked collaboratively to be present for each of them and support them in all of their interests and activities.

As any parent knows, school activities start early and tend to fill family schedules rapidly. Our family was no exception, and things really became chaotic when most of the kids were in high school. Anthony wrestled; Danie played softball and soccer; Ashley played basketball; and Mariah participated in track. And that was just the sports side of things!

We attended whatever we could whenever we could. Even though Christian was out of high school and his organized sports days were over, he did play on a Men's adult softball league, and we would go to watch him as well. We didn't limit ourselves to attending only the events of our biological children. From the beginning, they were all our kids, and we both did whatever we could to support them. We wanted them all to feel that unconditional support and love from both of us as much as possible.

We remained committed to continuing this approach as they went off to college. When Ashley played basketball in college in Kentucky, we both went to some of her games. When all three of the girls were in college, we made an effort to go and see each of them, even though they were attending in different states. We also visited Anthony when he was in the Marine Corps near Palm Springs. It was never calculated, and neither of us ever focused on only visiting our own biological children. Whenever we could plan a visit to see them, we did. Jeannette even went to see Mariah by herself when she was in college.

> **" We were intentional about making time for our own kids and created individualized time and experiences with our stepchildren. "**

Something we definitely did right was committing to spending time with each of the kids. We were intentional about making time for our own kids and created individualized time and experiences with our stepchildren. One-on-one quality time has always been a priority to stay closely connected. We still do that as much as we possibly can.

It gets harder as they get older and are married with families of their own. There is less time and it's important not to take them away from their spouses and kids. We try to make it happen as often as we can. I (Jeannette) know that when we are invited by the kids to do something, we always try to make it happen. We have to be more intentional as they have gotten older. Our kids are all different and have different likes and dislikes. We have tried to find things that they enjoy, that we can enjoy with them.

For example, Mariah and I (Jeannette) have enjoyed going out to dinner and to comedy shows. She loves comedy, and it is a good way for the two of us to get some time together. She will come over for dinner when Paul is out of town, and we will eat and watch a movie/show together. Sometimes just sitting outside on the deck and catching up is good.

Since Ashley lives out of state, it is harder to get that one-on-one quality time with her. However, when we go visit her family in Alaska, we have enjoyed going shopping together and out to lunch. Dinner or lunch dates are something I (Jeannette) have enjoyed and still enjoy with all of my kids. Quality time with

Danie has also included meeting up at a coffee shop and/or going shopping together. Intentionally being equally involved in the lives of your stepchildren is so important in successfully blending a family. Though it can sometimes feel like a balancing act, making sure all family members feel loved and supported is a delicate and essential part of the blending process.

I (Paul), after reflecting on the quality time I have spent with both my biological kids and step kids, I realized I need to be more intentional about seeking out time with them. Recently, I started to meet with the girls individually for coffee. I love getting together with both Mariah and Danie and finding out what is going on in their lives. No agenda—just connection. I have also gone to the gun shooting range individually with Christian and Anthony for some good male bonding time. Staying close with your adult kids is so important in growing and maintaining the blending of your family.

Give it and Them Time

As previously mentioned, we should have been engaged longer. Looking back, it's clear that the kids all could have benefitted from more time. Christian, Anthony, and Danie were still reeling from the divorce. Ashley and Mariah were getting to know yet another woman their dad was dating, plus her three kids.

Proceeding more slowly would have allowed them to get used to each of us as potential new stepparents and fully accept the idea of their parents remarrying. They also could have adjusted more smoothly to living with stepsiblings with more time to get to know them. It really was an enormous amount of adjustment for all of them in a fairly short span of time.

More time would have allowed us to incorporate more fun and non-threatening family experiences, like the game nights that we started after we were married. Looking back, incorporating more activities together like going to sporting events, skiing, snowmobiling, white-water rafting, and serving the homeless together would have helped us bond earlier as a family.

Family Time

Traveling together as a blended family is a great way to get to know one another well.

We prioritized quality time as a family and found this to be so beneficial. One way we did this was through travel. Traveling together as a blended family is a great way to get to know one another well. Family members are more likely to bond because everyone tends to relax and get out of their comfort zones. I (Paul) led mission groups to Mexico for many years, and we took the kids to Mexico with us several times. I have many friends there, and even before we were married, we took Danie, Mariah, and Ashley to Merida.

Danie and Mariah didn't really like each other on that first trip. They were probably fourteen and fifteen years old. That trip seemed to initiate a turning point in their relationship, even though developing their relationship was still a long road and process for them. It certainly wasn't a glamorous beach vacation, but we had a wonderful time. It's amazing how things like collaboratively helping those who are less fortunate and sleeping in a tiny house on hammocks can strengthen family bonds. We did a few touristy things as well.

We visited cenotes, which are basically sinkholes with beautiful fresh water at the bottom of them. Picture climbing down a ladder into a remote cave and swimming together in a uniquely beautiful setting. How many kids can say they've been to a cenote in the middle of a jungle? How many adults can?

That trip was good for Danie because she got to see a different side of me (Paul) and my girls. She saw that we were safe and that we liked to have fun and do cool, adventurous things.

The experiences we were blessed to enjoy were new for my kids and me (Jeannette). We were able to live adventurous lives, along with trying to do some good in the world. It was good for Danie, Christian, and Anthony to experience that. They learned and grew from their time at the orphanage in Mexico. We always packed crafts, toys, clothes, and all kinds of things for the needy children and their community. We also went to the Mayan ruins and then ended our trip in Cancun at the Marriott. My kids had never stayed anywhere like that.

When they were growing up, we didn't have a lot of money to travel. We took yearly vacations, but never out of the country. Christian and Danie love traveling to this day, and I know it's because we planted that seed when we traveled together as a blended family. It allowed us to experience new things together, laugh, and have fun. It provided excellent bonding time for our family.

We know we've been extremely blessed with the resources and ability to travel. Seeking out volunteer opportunities as a family, having game nights, and camping are inexpensive activities that are also great for family bonding.

Communication

Establishing and maintaining solid channels of communication with and between stepchildren is essential. I (Jeannette) always told my children that there wasn't anything they couldn't talk to me about, and we've both adopted that approach with all of the kids.

To truly build that trust, you have to be willing to withhold judgment and avoid harshly reprimanding them when they make mistakes. Again, we never forced communication between them (even though we may have had the urge occasionally with Danie and Mariah), but we've tried to be intentional about modeling open communication in our interactions with all of them and with each other. Even now, as adults, we all strive to be open and honest with each other. This sometimes leads to some difficult conversations and conflict but working our way through that conflict is ultimately what promotes growth and harmony.

Owning Mistakes and Offering Forgiveness

When you make a mistake, you have to own it. As parents, sometimes we don't think we need to apologize to our children, but we need to lead by example. This means being willing to apologize and then move on. We've learned that, even now, sometimes we may need to pause a conversation or debate until we can communicate without saying something we'll regret. Danie and I (Jeannette) argue/bicker all the time, but we are extremely close. We can have disagreements, speak our minds, and then let it go. Harboring resentment is pointless and can corrode even the strongest of relationships. In addition to being willing to apologize, forgiveness is key.

In stepfamilies, as in all families, chances are, somebody is going to get under your skin from time to time. You have to be willing and able to forgive. It may be easier with your own kids, but it is equally if not more important with someone else's kids.

> *You cannot harbor feelings or save up resentments to bring up in a subsequent disagreement; doing this only hinders growth and weakens bonds.*

When disagreements arise, you are bound to be hurt by words and actions that happen in the heat of those moments. As the parent and the adult, you have to be the bigger person and role model. You cannot harbor feelings or save up resentments to bring up in a subsequent disagreement; doing this only hinders growth and weakens bonds.

Of course, grace and forgiveness are key to the marital relationship as well. Jeannette is masterful at true forgiveness, which is really releasing the other person from pain and truly letting the indiscretion go. Just recently, I (Paul) crossed a boundary with her. I brought it up again a few weeks later, and she couldn't even remember what I was talking about. Now that's forgiveness!

Empty Nesting

In a traditional marriage, you have time together as a couple before you have children. We have never had that until now. Our house is quieter and more laid back, the bills are lower, and I (Jeannette) am learning to cook less. It is a big adjustment when you are accustomed to always having your kids, teens, then young adults around.

> **"**
> *We've tried to be intentional about making and taking time for and with each other throughout our marriage. It makes a difference.*
> **"**

Many parents and stepparents are afraid to be empty nesters. Some of them are afraid to be alone with each other because they have never been or if they had that time, it was so very long ago. This is why it is so important to take time to nurture your relationship when the kids are with you. Some people don't prioritize this or they plan to do it when the kids are grown and out of the house, but this can naturally create distance in the relationship. We've tried to be intentional about making and taking time for and with each other throughout our marriage. It makes a difference. Now that the kids are gone, we don't have to get reacquainted or make up for lost time. We're as close as we've ever been.

All but one of our children have come back to live with us for a time after they left at age eighteen. If you put off prioritizing your marriage until the kids are grown and gone, you could be setting yourselves up for some struggles. Some parents have this idea that they will have their kids at home for this set period of time, and then they will have quality time as a couple. The fact is that every child doesn't automatically leave home for good at age eighteen. It's important to discuss what your plans will be if and when the kids want or need to come back home for a period of time. You cannot say yes to one and no to another, so having a clear approach planned out ahead of time can prove very beneficial.

Steadfast Commitment and No Regrets

Jeannette and I were, and are, fiercely committed to each other; we went into this marriage knowing that divorce was not an option. When you commit to someone with kids, it absolutely cannot be an option. It's not just about you, so you have to be ready to put everything you've got into making it work. That being said, I (Paul) have never questioned my decision to get remarried. Not once. Even when things have been tough. Even when Danie was shooting me death stares or Anthony had legal trouble. I have never, ever had a single doubt.

I (Jeannette) had always longed for a relationship where my partner was my best friend, and I had been deprived of that in my first marriage. That's what Paul was and is to me. There's nobody else that I would rather spend time with than him. He knows everything about me, and I know everything about him. Not only is Paul my best friend, but he has been the best stepparent I could have ever wished for. Because he worked so hard to deal with the wounds from his past, he was able to become an amazing parent. He has never raised his voice or said a harsh word. He has been an amazing role model. I'm so grateful because that isn't something I had the privilege of growing up with, but it is something that I had desired so deeply for my own children.

It's the same for me (Paul). I have friends that I golf with who talk about the fact that they like to go golfing because they can get away from their wives. When I hear that, I just think, *I love being around my wife*. I play golf because it's fun, but rarely do I play eighteen holes. I'll take two hours to play nine holes, and then be happy to go home and tell her how I did. After all this time, she is still the person I want to share most of my time with.

What We've Learned

1. Take time to discuss how you will handle finances as a blended family before marriage. Within that discussion, commit to combining all resources rather than keeping them separate; become the "we" versus two individuals.

2. Discuss how financial support for children moving into independence will be handled in an equitable way.

3. Have some honest and deep discussion about your parenting styles and how they are alike and different. Decide how you will handle parenting as a couple. Clearly communicate this plan to your children.

4. Model and teach respect at all times. Don't assume that stepchildren will automatically respect you. Respect needs to be earned by all involved.

5. Consider family therapy and remember that even older children and young adults can benefit from that professional support.

6. Work hard to cultivate open and equal lines of communication.

7. Carve out plenty of time for building and strengthening relationships between each other and all of the kids. One-on-one time as well as quality family time are critical for creating and strengthening those lifetime bonds.

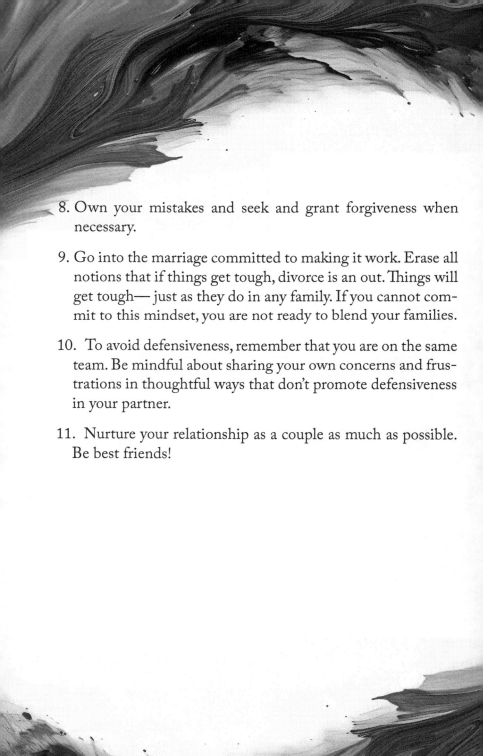

8. Own your mistakes and seek and grant forgiveness when necessary.

9. Go into the marriage committed to making it work. Erase all notions that if things get tough, divorce is an out. Things will get tough— just as they do in any family. If you cannot commit to this mindset, you are not ready to blend your families.

10. To avoid defensiveness, remember that you are on the same team. Be mindful about sharing your own concerns and frustrations in thoughtful ways that don't promote defensiveness in your partner.

11. Nurture your relationship as a couple as much as possible. Be best friends!

Part Four

The Spices of our Lives

Seven

Meet the Kids

Christian

As a child, I never imagined my parents getting divorced. As a young adult getting ready to navigate college and explore my own identity, I suddenly found myself part of a blended family with a new stepparent and stepsiblings. We all had to learn new routines, adapt to new expectations, and attempt to form bonds with our new family members. Inevitably, there were some conflicts along the way.

Over time, we've all learned to appreciate the unique qualities of each member of our family. We've learned to support each other through the challenges life throws at us, celebrate each other's achievements, and genuinely enjoy being together. Like any journey, ours began with some unpredictability.

My experiences with my parents' divorce were very different from that of my siblings because of my age at the time. I was a senior in high school. It was somewhat surprising when they initially separated because they never fought in front of us.

However, I *had* noticed that they were sleeping in separate beds, so I knew something was up. The fact that we never saw them fighting probably made the divorce a bit harder to deal with, at least for me at that age. I grew up with married parents for seventeen or eighteen years. Then suddenly, it was like, "Hey I'm ready to go to college, and now my parents are getting divorced." I'm not sure if it felt disturbing or just strange. After the divorce, my relationships with each of my parents stayed pretty much the same; the only big difference was that they had two separate households.

> " Throughout the separation and divorce, I made an effort to check in on my siblings. I tried to be there for them as much as I could "

Throughout the separation and divorce, I made an effort to check in on my siblings. I tried to be there for them as much as I could. I went to the *Colorado School of Mines* and was playing football, so I was quite busy. I probably wasn't there for them as much as I could have been, but I wanted to consistently check in on them and make sure they were okay. My school was only twenty minutes away from home, so I came home for the weekends sometimes, and that was a good way to check in and stay connected.

I don't recall if I met Paul before our two families all met. I do remember my mom sitting us all down and telling us about him. It didn't surprise or upset me; I wanted my mom to be happy. When we all met at the bowling alley, Danie and Mariah acted differently than the rest of us, which was to be expected because they were the youngest. They were both very quiet, and Mariah was super clingy with her dad. Knowing the backstory of Paul and his ex-wife, as well as the struggles Mariah and Ashley went through with their mom, the way they acted makes sense. My first impression of Paul was that he was a little strange. He was very outgoing and talkative, and sometimes, I wondered where he was pulling the things he would talk about from. His personality was very different from what I was used to.

On the day that we all met, and in the days and weeks that followed, I was okay just letting the situation unfold. I saw Mariah become attached to my mom as time went on. She never had that motherly figure with her mom, so she seemed to appreciate having that with my mom. I remember Danie being very jealous as a kid, and it's taken a long time for her to get over that. I was a young adult, and I figured my mother was an adult and single, and she had every right to start dating. I thought it was fine for her to move on with her life.

When everyone moved in together right before my mom married Paul, it didn't really faze me. I was living in Golden, Colorado at that time. Later, when I transferred from the *School of Mines* to *Metropolitan State* in 2008, I ended up moving back in with them. There was an unfinished basement, and my mom put up a sheet down there to give me some privacy within the crowded house that was our new normal. I will say it was a big adjustment to live there with everyone. I went from having one sister to three, and they were all younger. I was working full-time and going to school so wasn't around that much, but it was still a bit difficult to get used to living with three people I'd never lived with before.

I eventually started to see different sides of Paul, which I may not have seen had I not lived there. He wasn't just a talkative, quirky guy anymore. He would get mad occasionally and sternly parent his girls when they needed redirection.

Paul and my mom had very different parenting styles. I know they tried to only discipline their own biological kids at first. I remember listening to Danie and Anthony have conversations with my mom about how Ashley and Mariah could do certain things that were unacceptable for them to do. I don't think there was as much of that as there could have been, but it went on, most likely on both sides.

It did take me a while to truly see who Paul was as a person. I just kind of sat back for a time and watched how he treated my mom and how he treated Danie, Anthony, and me. He really opened his arms and treated us just like he treated Ashley and Mariah. We were all treated like his kids. It took a few years for me to see that, but it's something I really appreciate and respect.

I'm an easy-going person and always have been. I look at things like *if they are meant to be, they'll be*. If Paul hadn't been a nice guy, that would have come out, and I would have spoken up about it at that time. If they hadn't been meant to be, something would have occurred to make me see that. Withholding judgment and watching him with my mom and siblings allowed our relationship to take root.

Paul and my mom did many things well as they were blending our families. One thing they did (and still do) well to help us grow together as a family was to coordinate family events and always include everyone. There was no obvious separation of family members for certain events. Birthday dinners, even to this day, happen for everyone. We all vacationed together whenever possible, and that provided prime opportunities to bond. They also each made it a point to do special things with each of us. For example, Paul would take Anthony and me to baseball games to connect with us and build our relationships, and my mom would take the girls to get their nails done. They did their best to make it all less awkward from the start and to make everyone feel welcome and loved. My wife and I started dating in high school, and she was always included and treated as part of the family as well.

> Looking back, there aren't many things I can think of that Paul and my mother could have done better.

Looking back, there aren't many things I can think of that Paul and my mother could have done better. One thing that both Anthony and I struggled with was seeing Mariah, Ashley, and Danie encouraged to go to college out of state. Paul and my mom paid for big chunks of their college so that they could afford to do that.

Anthony went into the military, but he would have most likely been afforded the same opportunity. Because of my age and situation, I ended up having to pay for all of my college tuition myself. Times were just different. Seeing others afforded different opportunities did cause a ripple effect within some of the relationships. There were also more trips taken with Mariah and Danie, again, mostly due to timing and the different stages that we were in our lives. These are really minor issues, though, in the grand scheme of things.

Today, I see us all as one big family. My relationships with Paul and Mariah are a bit closer than my relationship with Ashley, but that is mainly because we haven't spent as much time together. When I moved into the house with everyone, she was going off to college; now she lives in Alaska. I see Mariah as my little sister. She's been part of my life longer than she hasn't.

My relationship with Paul has gotten better with time. If I need something, I know I can always sit down and talk with him about it. When there is an occasional minor tiff with my mom, he will sit and listen and keep an open mind. It's never just one-sided where he automatically agrees with my mom. He'll give his honest opinion. He'll tell her if he thinks she is wrong, just like he'll tell me if he thinks I'm wrong. I appreciate and respect that so much.

My relationship with my dad remains the same. I was finished with college and about to get married when he moved to Wyoming. It became a bit more difficult to include him in everything and still is today because he lives in a different state. My wife's mother lives in Wyoming as well. Now that we have two kids, it is a bit difficult sometimes. We want to try to include them in everything, but they did choose to live in a different state, so they may not always have the same amount of inclusion as those living closer to us. In retrospect, in the beginning of my mom's relationship with Paul, I may have been a little protective of my dad, but it was nothing out of the ordinary. If the relationship between my mom and Paul or Paul and any of us bothered him, he never showed it. I appreciate that our parents are all able to be around each other, and there has never been any visible fighting between them. That made and still makes everything easier on all of us, especially now that I have my own kids.

Since my wife's parents are also divorced and remarried, my kids are lucky enough to have four grandfathers and four grand-mothers. To say they are spoiled would be an understatement. It's pretty amazing to have Paul willing and able to jump in and help with them, and I know my mom does the same for Ashley when possible. When my wife took my mom out recently for Mother's Day, Paul didn't hesitate to watch the boys for us, which is so awesome.

My advice to anyone preparing to blend families is to keep an open mind. I've also learned, later in life, that open communication for everyone involved is crucial. If you don't feel comfortable saying what you need to say, that is when relationships suffer. Building up the trust necessary to have open conversations is key. Parents, be ready and willing to listen without judgment or backlash. That's something that my mother did well from the beginning. I've always felt comfortable talking honestly with her because she instilled that into all of us early in our lives. Now I am lucky to have that with Paul as well. I could go to either one of them and say what's on my mind, and I know that they would both listen and give honest feedback. I know I'm lucky to have that kind of relationship with each of them.

Like any family, we've had our issues and some ups and downs, but overall, we have honest, authentic relationships and a net-work of strong bonds. As a parent of two young children my-self, I'm grateful for the lessons I've learned from being part of a blended family. I deeply understand the importance of open communication and compromise in any relationship, and I've seen the positive impact of the hard work my mother and Paul put in to create a strong sense of unity and belonging. All of this has allowed us to grow as individuals and become a strong family unit.

I know that there will continue to be changes within relationships and hurdles to overcome. I am confident that the unique blend of personalities and experiences that make up who we are will help us navigate those hurdles and continue to grow as individuals and as a family.

My advice to anyone preparing to blend families is to keep an open mind. I've also learned, later in life, that open communication for everyone involved is crucial. If you don't feel comfortable saying what you need to say, that is when relationships suffer.

Ashley

Experiencing the divorce of my parents and the blending of my new family helped mold me into who I am today as a daughter, sibling, spouse, and even as a person, but especially as a parent. Looking back on my childhood, some memories are vivid, and many are blurry. As an adult, I'm more appreciative than ever that my dad found his way, and that he and Jeannette found each other.

Memories of my parents being happy together in my early years are rare to non-existent. My mother was a very angry woman, and it was clear, even to me as a kid, that the relationship that she and my dad had was not healthy. News of their separation and subsequent divorce came more as a relief than anything else to me. It was a brutal divorce, with nonstop fighting between them. The toll it took on my dad, both emotionally and financially, was immense. Some of it I realized at the time, but I learned more about the severity of it much later, once we all had come through it and were better able to process what had happened from the other side.

After the divorce, my sister and I were splitting time with my mom and dad in their separate settings and lives. We started going to therapy, and eventually, when more of the truth seeped out, my mom was deemed unfit to have custody of us. My dad was finally granted full custody. I was so grateful for that. We did not see our mother for six months after custody was granted, then she was allowed supervised visitation. After that, we were given the choice to spend time with her.

Since she blamed me for her loss of custody, I chose to spend less time with her than my sister, Mariah, did. I visited her, but never spent the night. I was in seventh grade and almost six years older than Mariah. At her young age, she naturally chose to spend more time with our mother. When she was home with me and my dad, I instinctively stepped into a motherly role with her. Although our relationship is different today, it is stronger than ever. We don't live near each other, but we talk at least once every week.

> **"** *Therapy helped me manage my emotions and navigate my shifting circumstances and relationships* **"**

Dealing with all of the drama, change, and issues with my mother was difficult. Therapy helped me manage my emotions and navigate my shifting circumstances and relationships. I voluntarily continued with it for at least four years, and it was the best thing I could have ever done. My mother was an abusive alcoholic and extremely manipulative. I knew I never wanted to be like her, and I had a lot of trauma and emotion to work through. Like my dad, I did EMDR, and it was life-altering and empowering for me. It was comforting to see my dad making positive strides as well.

When my dad started dating other people, I was happy and excited for him. I knew that he deserved to be happy and loved, and I really wanted that for him. There were only two women that he introduced us to before Jeannette. I know now that he was very intentional about not introducing us to every woman he dated. Until he knew a woman well and felt there was potential for a serious relationship to develop, he didn't even consider bringing her into our lives. I admire that wisdom and can just imagine the turmoil and heartbreak he likely spared us by being cautious. I adopted that very rule as my own after I had my daughter and became a single mother trying to navigate the dating scene.

When my sister and I learned about Jeannette and her kids, it really didn't bother me. Again, I wanted my dad to be happy, and I trusted him and his judgment. A meeting of the two families was scheduled shortly thereafter. As previously mentioned, it took place at a bowling alley. It was super awkward, and in terms of potential blending, we all seemed to be a concoction that was not going to mix well. Our two families sat on separate sides and didn't appear to have anything in common at first glance. I was sixteen, and Mariah was in that awkward middle school phase.

Jeannette was pretty and kind, but her kids were very standoffish with us. I do recall Christian's girlfriend (now his wife), Heather, being friendly and the only one who even attempted to talk to me and Mariah. She was and still is the mediator of the family. Danie was clearly not happy. That girl knew how to glare through your soul, and that's just what she did.

As uncomfortable as that first meeting was, my perspective has shifted from bitterness to a place of understanding. After all, my parents had been divorced since I was in middle school, and I was used to my dad dating. It wasn't that crazy of a situation for me, but it was a drastic adjustment for all of them. Their parents' separation was more recent, and the wounds were fresh while ours were scarred over and numb. We were all going through very different things at that time, and we were kids.

As the relationship between my dad and Jeannette continued to develop, they brought us all together at least once per week throughout that first year. I knew early on that I liked Jeannette better than the other two serious girlfriends my dad had introduced us to. It was obvious that she was good for my dad, and she made him extremely happy. And, as a bonus, her kids played sports, so she understood my passion for basketball as well as what was involved in being a student-athlete. She was also an excellent listener, and that was new for me. She didn't try to force her way into a relationship with me or my sister; she worked hard to build rapport with each of us in meaningful ways.

When it was time to come together and live under the same roof, I was mostly fine with it. Right after the wedding, when my dad and Jennette went on their honeymoon, I stayed alone in the new, empty house for a week. It's a pretty vivid memory for me, probably because I was creeped out. The new house was three stories with an unfinished basement. I probably only went upstairs once the entire time! When everyone settled in, I ended up sharing half of the basement with Christian for part of the time. I was a senior in high school and busy with basketball and work, so I was gone a lot. When I was home, I was often busy with homework because I had transferred to a very demanding prep school for the last two years of high school. So, the act of formally blending our families by moving in together didn't really faze me. I did my own thing; as a typical teenager, I cared mostly about myself.

There were a few rocky moments as we all adjusted; some that we laugh about today, and some that we've never spoken of since. Before we moved in together, I had been used to being on my own. When Mariah would go to my mom's, and my dad was traveling, I stayed home alone and had my own schedule. I'm not sure exactly how healthy or productive that was. After all, I was a teenager. When Jeannette became another parental figure in my life, her routines and schedules were completely foreign to me, and having someone call the shots for me when my dad was gone really threw me off. This was a minor annoyance compared to dealing with Danie.

From that first meeting at the bowling alley, Danie was difficult to deal with. She was extremely vocal about her disapproval of my dad and Jeannette, and that complicated things. I grew frustrated with her quickly because I saw her as a brat causing more chaos than necessary. She and Anthony fought constantly, and things were terrible between her and Mariah for at least four years.

Mariah struggled with social skills and was slower to develop when we were kids. She didn't know how to handle her emotions in healthy ways. I recall her biting Danie at one point in a fit of rage. I understand now, as an adult and parent myself, that they were both so much younger than the rest of us and dealing with trauma in their own ways. Their experiences were vastly different due to where they were developmentally.

As I rummage through my memories for the most trying aspects of blending our families, there is one that pops sharply into view. I'm guessing it is so strong because of my aversion to conflict, but also because of who Jeannette was becoming in my life and is to me today. I was working on an essay for school, and Anthony was supposed to have done the dishes but hadn't. Jeannette came in and asked him about it, and he went off on her. My fury grew as I listened to him yell horrific things at her about how useless she was, and how she never did anything around the house. I mean it was the furthest thing from the truth; Jeannette is basically a modern-day Betty Crocker. I finally exploded. With tears pooling in my eyes, I let him have it. I roared at him about how disrespectful he was being and how utterly wrong he was. I ranted that he needed to appreciate her; he had no idea how lucky he was to have her. I would've given anything to have grown up with a mom like her, and his behavior disgusted me. When I was finished, breathless and exhausted, I recall Jeannette and Anthony standing speechless, staring at me for what felt like forever. Anthony then walked away and ignored me for the next three days. He never spoke to Jeannette that way in my presence again.

Except for that explosion at Anthony, my relationship with him was and is fine. He had a bit of an attitude when we were growing up, and he was one to always say what he thought. I think he got a lot of crap when we were kids because he is a talker, and school was harder for him. He's still a talker, but he's matured so much.

Christian and I always got along well. I am a peacekeeper and hate conflict, and I think Christian is the same way. We were the older siblings and took on that caretaker role with our younger sisters, so we had that in common. We both were forced to grow up and be more mentally mature earlier than the average kid. One amazing connection my husband and I now share with Christian and Heather is that our kids are literally best friends when they are together. We each have two children and they are all very close in age. We just went on a family vacation a few weeks ago, and it was amazing. We loved getting to know Christian and Heather better on the cruise and sharing the joys and perils of parenthood.

I realize now that those one-on-one experiences were intentional, and I so appreciate that.

Jeannette was easy to get to know and love. She was a wonderful listener and so supportive. It was obvious that she worked hard to build authentic relationships with each of us, just like my dad did with Anthony, Christian, and Danie. Some of my most treasured times with her were one-on-one, driving to get Starbucks. I realize now that those one-on-one experiences were intentional, and I so appreciate that. I didn't grow up with a strong mother figure, and although we were both cautious at first, she has beautifully filled that role in my life.

Today, each relationship in our blended family is unique. I am close to Mariah, and we connect by phone often. Anthony and I get along well. We have genuine respect for each other and enjoy visiting when I am home, but we don't call or text each other. We aren't friends; we are siblings. My relationship with Christian is similar. He has always been level-headed, non-confrontational, and easy-going, and we have that in common. Heather has always been part of the family as well. At times, she was the biggest reason I enjoyed going back home. If there was drama, we could always depend on her to be the mediator. She has always been willing to help everyone, and she is the one person I can always talk to when everybody else in the family is driving me crazy. I consider Jeannette both a mother and a friend.

Danie and I still have very different perspectives on things, but I have a ton of respect for her. She has worked hard to become a nurse after switching directions a time or two in college. I admire her dedication and determination. Because of the age difference between us, our views on many things will likely always vary, but I think that is natural and perfectly fine.

I do see us as one big successfully blended family. We all get along and try to spend time together when we can. I live in Alaska, so I don't see everyone as often as they see each other. When I come home, things are pleasant and natural—worlds away from what they were on that day long ago at the bowling alley.

If I had to give advice to others preparing to blend, there are many positive experiences I can and do draw from. I now have a blended family of my own. My husband has two sons from his previous marriage, and my daughter was born before I met him. We also have one son together. My experience has been positive, and I attribute much of that to what I've learned from my dad and Jeannette. My stepsons were in high school when I met their dad. I was twenty-seven years old, and they were teenagers. I was closer in age to them than I was to their dad. My husband, Rob, was devastated by his divorce, and as I had with my dad, his boys saw that. They wanted him to find peace and happiness, and I think they saw him find that with me. They are now in their twenties.

When Rob and I brought our families together, we were determined to act as one family, not two separate units. Later, when our son was born, we were intentional about spending time with the older kids away from the younger ones and making them each feel special and loved just as Jeannette and my dad had done with me and my siblings. We also adopted the policy of disciplining our own biological children in the beginning of the relationship, and that worked well. One of the things that helped me feel connected as a child was the routine of having dinner together each evening and talking about each person's day. Developing the habit of really listening and interacting about our days is a cherished memory for me and one that I have adopted and enjoyed as a parent.

One thing that we are careful to avoid is comparing our kids. I recall Jeannette once saying to Anthony, "Why can't you be more like Ashley?" My dad stopped her in her tracks and explained that it wasn't right to compare us. He was right. Making comparisons only creates self-doubt and animosity. I'm sure this is true in any family, but I imagine it can be especially devastating when comparing stepsiblings. We've been intentional about not comparing our older sons to each other or to their younger siblings.

Bringing everyone together as a family as much as possible is important and something Jeannette and my dad have done a great job with while we were growing up and now that we are all adults. Again, we recently enjoyed a family cruise, and it was a wonderful experience. I try to emulate that with my blended family, too, and pull us all together as much as possible.

I know my dad is very proud of how everything has turned out, and he should be. We all have successful and impactful careers that we pursued and worked hard for. I am a teacher. Anthony is a chef. Danie is a nurse, Mariah does stand-up comedy and manages a restaurant, and Christian is a police officer. I know that our lives could have been vastly different had we been unable to successfully blend as a family. It took a lot of skill, patience, and insight from my dad and Jeannette, and an abundance of compromise from all of us. With vastly different personalities and interests, we all had to learn to accept and appreciate each other. I think we have been able to do that and experience invaluable personal growth and fulfillment along the way.

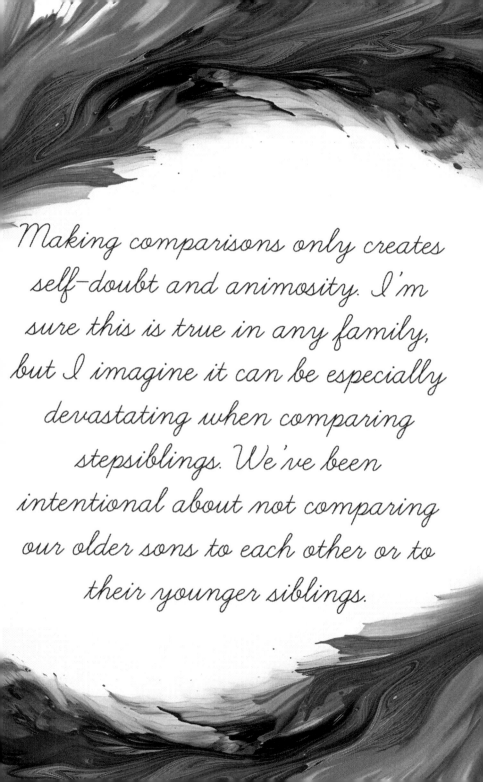

Making comparisons only creates self-doubt and animosity. I'm sure this is true in any family, but I imagine it can be especially devastating when comparing stepsiblings. We've been intentional about not comparing our older sons to each other or to their younger siblings.

Anthony

I was in eighth grade when my parents initially separated. The separation was pretty much a total surprise to me at the time. Right before my ninth-grade year began, they made it clear that they were proceeding with a divorce. By that point, I expected it. The next big surprise that came my way was Paul.

My mom didn't tell us that she was dating or even thinking about dating, so it was a bit of a shock to my siblings and me when we finally found out she was in a relationship with someone other than our dad. She didn't realize it, but I did have an inkling something was going on before she officially told us about Paul. I was going to stay with my dad one night and had forgotten something at home. When I went back to the house to get it, there was a strange car outside the house. It was one of those surreal moments where you notice something is off, but just let it slide and continue what you're doing. I found out years later that she had hidden him downstairs in the basement when she saw that I was back. I'm not sure if I thought it was funny at the time, but the irony of the parent trying to hide her boyfriend from her teenage son is pretty funny to me now.

We officially learned about Paul and his family when I was in tenth grade. We met them shortly after. My mom had tried to keep it from us for a bit, and I remember wishing that she would have let us know about him a little sooner. The transition from finding out about him and meeting Paul and his daughters could have gone smoother if we'd had more time to come to terms with the fact that she was dating. I vaguely remember going and meeting everybody at the bowling alley. Our mom had prepped us, and we knew we would meet Ashley and Mariah at the same time. It didn't feel that strange to me at the time; it just all felt a bit rushed. I think I may have been looking at things a bit more logically than my siblings, though.

Things moved rapidly after that first meeting, and before we knew it, Paul and my mom were married. After the wedding, we all lived in the same house for a year. I was very block-headed, immature, and stubborn when I was younger. I recall that Ashley and I didn't gel initially. Our personalities clashed when we were suddenly living under the same roof. Our relationship took a positive turn probably six years ago or so, when we both became older and more mature. Whether intentionally or just instinctively, my mom and Paul did several things to help Ashley and I, and really all of us, build relationships.

I am grateful that they never pushed us or tried to rush the relationship-building. They were diligent about allowing Paul to earn our respect. They let us warm up to and accept Paul and gave Ashley and Mariah time to warm up to my mom. They let us form connections with each other in our own time instead of trying to force them. I do have friends who are in blended families, and they do not like their stepsiblings and/or stepparents, so I know that things could have been a lot different had they tried to force things prematurely.

One thing Paul did on his own to build trust with us was to take a genuine interest in us as individuals. He never made it feel like he was obligated to take an interest because we were his wife's kids. He truly took the time to get to know us. One time, I remember we ended up wrestling in our living room. I don't know how it got started, but I recall that my mom didn't stop us like she would have if it had been me and my siblings wrestling. Looking back, I'm sure she was too happy to see us bonding to interrupt the fun.

I'm sure discipline can be an issue in stepfamilies. My mom and Paul had a good approach to discipline, especially early in the relationship. I think they remained consistent in how they each approached discipline before getting together. They were cautious about not trying to intervene too much as stepparents right away. That's not to say that Paul kept quiet when he thought I needed guidance or redirection. He has stepped up and given it to me straight before, and I appreciate that. Because we have a solid relationship, I am always open to listening to what he has to say. I respect him and know that if he has questions or advice for me, it all comes from a place of caring.

From the beginning of their relationship, I felt loved and supported by both of them, even when I wasn't my most mature self. I think they did a great job of making us all feel that equally. I don't recall ever feeling jealous or that anything was handled unfairly. Danie was the baby of the family, so she got the baby of the family treatment, but I think that most likely happens in all families.

Since my relationship with my dad was rocky, I was the first child that my mom introduced to therapy. I was in high school when I started it. It did improve my relationship with him, but the added benefit was that it improved my relationships with everyone else as well. If my siblings were also seeing therapists at the time, I didn't know about it. I do wish they would have pushed a little harder to keep me in it when I decided to stop going. I'm sure they didn't want to force me (or any of us), but I do think it would have been better if they had encouraged all of us to engage in therapy on an ongoing basis. Therapy changed my life in general. It has helped me in all aspects of my life, and I still do it. I believe that everyone can benefit from it. For children of divorce, it can be a game-changer.

Paul stopped being my stepdad and became my dad when I was a senior in high school. It was regionals for wrestling and my final event. My mom and Paul drove four and a half hours to be there and support me. His willingness to come all that way to watch me was really a game-changer for my relationship with him. Our bond had been growing for a while, but he truly became a second dad to me that day. It became clear that he truly had my back, not just as a stepdad, but as a parent.

Because my dad and I didn't have the greatest relationship to begin with, accepting Paul and the situation may have been a bit easier for me than it was for Danie. She had a hard time with the whole idea of Paul being with our mom and our families coming together. My intention was to try to help her, but my efforts didn't pay off. I recall that whenever I tried to intervene, it turned into an argument between the two of us. Personally, I had more issues adjusting to my new siblings than to Paul. As I already mentioned, I was immature at the time, and I'm sure that was the root of many of those issues.

My dad had nothing against Paul, but I do think he was a bit insecure around him at first. However he may have been feeling, he never spoke poorly of Paul, and I am truly grateful for that. My wife recently asked me why I still called Paul my stepdad because we are so close now. I had to think about that for a minute. Since I do have a relationship with my dad, I realize that I am lucky enough to really have two dads. I think I refer to Paul as my stepdad as a courtesy to my dad and to give context to people. I would never want my dad to feel any sort of hurt or resentment or that he has been replaced in any way because he hasn't.

It's important to remember that your parent's happiness is just as important as yours.

Reflecting on how our families blended, the biggest piece of advice I'd give individuals who are having trouble accepting a stepparent is to remember it isn't just about you. It's about your mom or dad and their happiness. I remember this being difficult for Danie, especially at her young age. She didn't really like anybody that my dad was dating either. It's important to remember that your parent's happiness is just as important as yours.

Today, I do think of all of us as one big family. I don't see or think about any type of line or separation. We still get together for family dinners and game nights, and it's great. If we couldn't do that, I'm sure we wouldn't all see each other as one big family as much as we do. We also have the opportunity to vacation together. I understand that this is a blessing that our family has, and that all families might not have the same opportunities. Spending this quality time together is invaluable. It allows us to create lasting memories, but more importantly, solidify our family bonds.

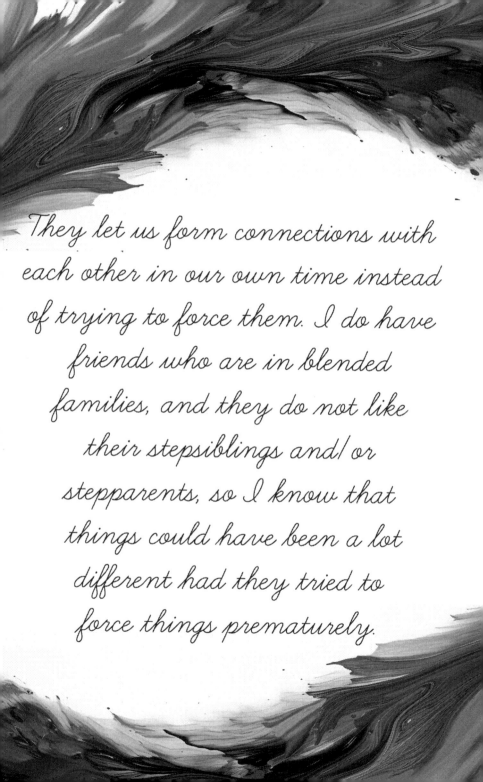

They let us form connections with each other in our own time instead of trying to force them. I do have friends who are in blended families, and they do not like their stepsiblings and/or stepparents, so I know that things could have been a lot different had they tried to force things prematurely.

Mariah

My childhood memories are a patchwork of different stages, each with its own distinct color. I remember the tension with my biological parents before they divorced, the freedom to be a child with my dad and Jeannette after they married, and the roller-coaster of emotions that came with gaining new siblings. These experiences have all contributed to who I am today, and although my family tree is anything but typical, I've grown to love its shape and size.

> **"**
>
> *I honestly don't have many good memories of them together before the divorce.*
>
> **"**

I was seven or eight when my parents separated and didn't even truly know what divorce was. I lived in a small town and divorce wasn't common at that time. Even though I was young, I did recognize that my parents didn't like each other very much, so I can't say their separation came as a surprise. What was a surprise was how long they actually stayed together. At one point, I remember that my mom was sleeping in the closet; they had a big walk-in closet, and she slept on an air mattress in there. My dad slept on the bed. That was a pretty good indicator, even to seven-year-old me, that they weren't getting along. I honestly don't have many good memories of them together before the divorce. This, in itself, seems to be a testament to the toxicity of their relationship.

My parents handled the divorce in very different ways. My dad went one direction, and my mom went the other. My dad did not really tell me anything except what I absolutely needed to know, like the logistics of how things were going to work. He didn't tell us about the unhinged things my mom was doing behind the scenes until we were much older.

Ashley and I became my mom's counselors and support system, though we were way too young to be doing that. I had no idea at the time what my dad was going through because he refused to burden me with it; he just let me be a kid. Thinking and talking about it all still makes me extremely emotional. When I'm reflecting, I do try to find the bright spots within my memories of that time.

When I found out that my dad was dating, it wasn't that big of a deal to me. It wasn't that difficult to win me over as a kid. I talked to pretty much everybody. It wasn't (and still isn't) hard for me to make friends. If you made me food or got me a gift or something, you were in. My dad never gave me warnings about the women he was seeing or anything, and I never felt like I needed that.

So, Jeannette entered my life without much fanfare, and that was just fine with me. I remember that we were moving from our house, and she came over to help. We packed my closet, then played *Uno Attack*. I had both help with packing and positive attention from a lovely, kind woman AND there was no drama. It was a win-win-win for me!

When it was time to meet her kids, I'd been through that routine a few times with others already; it wasn't the first time my dad had dated someone with kids. To me, it was just like, *Oh, okay, more people to meet and talk to.* All of Jeannette's kids seemed to have a much harder time with it. That makes sense because all of the drama and change with their parents was so recent for them. I was like, *My parents have hated each other for years, so, let's get this moving!*

Our worlds collided at a bowling alley. I can still picture Ashley and I on one lane with my dad and Jeannette. Everyone else was on the other lane. I had no clue at the time, but Danie always talks about how she remembers exactly what we were wearing, and that she hated us and was glaring at us. I have zero recollection of any of that. My version of the memory goes like this: *We went bowling, and we had fun. It was great!* I had no idea anyone didn't enjoy it until many years later, probably after my dad and Jeannette got married.

As my dad and Jeannette continued to date, I knew there was something different about Jeannette compared to the other women my dad had been in serious relationships with. I got along with all of them, but I could tell that my dad had a stronger attachment to Jeannette. I always knew that they would end up getting married. I was so positive about this that I would always refer to Danie as my future stepsister in conversations with my friends. She would have been mortified had she known. As fate would have it, we did become stepsisters a short time later.

A few weeks before the wedding, we all moved in together. There is no negativity surrounding that memory for me. Personally, I was ready for it. I was like, *Let's do this!* I have two older brothers from my mom's first marriage, and I get along fine with them, but we aren't close. Before my parents got divorced, they had already moved out of the house completely. They were much older, so we basically lived separate lives and completely different childhoods.

So, when my dad and Jeannette planned to marry, I thought, *We'll have more siblings, and that's awesome!* On their wedding day, I rode in the same car and had to get in the backseat with Danie. After the wedding, I was like, "Scoot over sister!" I think she may have glared a hole into the seat in front of her at that point.

The relationships with my new siblings developed in unique ways and at different rates. If what we were doing was attempting to blend, the blender was broken when it came to Danie and me. We didn't even talk for a long time. She was upset that her mom married my dad, and I was upset that she didn't want any type of relationship with me. That animosity kept building until we got to a point where we did not talk to each other unless we absolutely had to. It was also just a weird dynamic for me; it was the first time I wasn't the youngest child. We were only fourteen months apart, and there was definitely a youngest-child power struggle going on.

I do remember that one of the few things that we connected about was *America's Next Top Model.* We weren't allowed to watch it, so when our parents were gone, we'd look at each other and say, "It's time!" then sit together on the couch and watch it. Maybe the blender wasn't broken, and the blades were just dull? Nothing like some good reality television to facilitate the process of finding out.

Outside of the house, Danie and I did not even remotely act or look like siblings, or even acquaintances, for that matter. Although we were both fairly involved and well-known at school, people had no idea we were related. Danie was involved in sports, and I was the school mascot, involved in a volunteer club, and on the student council. We both knew a lot of people, but unless someone came to the house, nobody even knew that we knew each other. Only our very close friends knew we were siblings.

Vacationing together helped Danie and I get to know each other. I think my parents knew this and were strategic, but not obvious or dramatic about making it happen. There was a specific trip we took to Mexico that had a positive impact on our relationship. I had already been there many times with my dad, but we went with Jeannette and Danie that particular time. I remember spending a lot of time with Danie and really getting to know her during that trip. When you are in a strange place where you don't know anyone, you will gravitate toward familiarity. That's what Danie and I would do on a lot of those trips, and it helped us form an authentic connection.

The summer before I went to college in Seattle, we visited my future school together. Danie and I had a defining moment at the airport. She asked me for a piece of gum, and I told her she could only have one if she told me that she loved me. So, she did it. She told me she loved me. Although it meant so much to me, I wanted to keep the moment lighthearted, so I nonchalantly thanked her and tossed her the gum.

"With some time and space, we were able to better appreciate each other and form a healthier relationship.

Looking back, I honestly think it took Danie and I living apart to learn to truly accept and respect each other. We probably shouldn't live together again. We have very different personalities, but what we have in common is that both of us like to be in control. Growing up in the same house, there was often a silent tug-of-war raging in the background with two emotional teenagers trying to win control in their unique ways. Going our separate ways and off to college positively changed our relationship. With some time and space, we were able to better appreciate each other and form a healthier relationship. I'm pretty sure the maturity we each gained with time and experience was helpful as well!

My relationship with Anthony was different from the start. I've never been great at writing in my diary because my attention span is short, but there were some random days that I did write in my diary because of moments that had a profound impact on me. I recently found a page where I wrote that Anthony gave me a hug on my thirteenth birthday. It would have been the summer after my parents (my dad and Jeannette) got married, and he had given me a hug for the first time. It makes me tear up to think about it because I just love him so much. Anthony and I are tight. We lived together for almost a year during COVID. We had an apartment together but had completely different schedules. That's when I learned that he's a night owl, and I'm a morning person. We always laugh about the fact that we never saw each other during the first month of sharing the apartment. We really were like ships passing in the night. Living with him during that time confirmed and strengthened the bond we had already formed.

I've never felt super close to Christian. He was in college when our parents got married, so he was already out living his own life. The biggest thing we were able to bond over when I got older was the fact that I wanted to be in law enforcement. He was a police officer, and I was a probation officer for a while in the same department as him. I had the chance to do a ride-along with him and learn the ins and outs of his job. Today, we get along just fine. I'm not exactly going to call him to talk about my week or anything like that, but I'll go over to his house and hang out with his family.

Ashley and I continue to have a special bond because of our shared experiences with my mom and that other part of our childhood. Danie, Anthony, and Christian also experienced their parents' divorce and split time with their dad and Jeannette and my dad, but it was different. Even though they faced the same challenges that come with parents divorcing, the transition from home to home for Danie, Anthony, and Christian was not as drastic as it was for us. Understandably, it would be difficult for them to truly empathize with us because of what we went through with our mom.

My relationship with my dad has remained constant throughout my life. I am literally the female version of him, so I completely understand the way he thinks. We think so similarly that it sometimes really freaks me out. Not only do we have similar thinking patterns, but we also share many of the same habits and conflict resolution approaches; it's bizarre!

Ashley and Christian both have kids of their own now, and one thing I love about our blended family is having these amazing little nieces and nephews. All the young kids have great nicknames for me, and it's so fun. To them, we are all aunts and uncles. There is no blending process, and the word *step* isn't part of their vocabularies. I tend to think about Danie, Christian, and Anthony in the same way; It doesn't matter if I'm blood-related to them or not. I think of and refer to all of them as my siblings.

Jeannette was easy to develop a relationship with. She didn't try to fake or force relationships with us. It never felt like she was trying to step in as our new mom and boss us around. It did take some getting used to because Jeannette is extremely different from my biological mother. At first, I just saw her as a really nice lady. It's clear now that she was intentional about building a relationship with me. I always knew she was not trying to replace my mom but authentically wanted to support me and be a positive figure in my life. She was determined to show her care and concern in a genuine way and took the initiative to foster a relationship with me that felt like a bonus, not an obligation.

There were only a few specific moments when I poked the bear. I don't even remember what I was trying to test her on, but she passed. For the most part, I got along with my dad and Jeannette well. What was difficult was that I was living two different childhoods at the same time. Right after the divorce, Ashley and I were with just my mom for like three to six months. Then we started going back and forth between my mom and dad. At one point, a counselor asked my sister if she had been abused by my mom and she said yes. That was when the court said that we would stay with my dad. I don't know what my mom had to do to regain some of her parental rights, but there were six months of just living with my dad. I believe it was during that time that I met Jeannette. My dad, Jeannette, and Ashley lived together full time and I went to my mom's for half of the time.

Honestly, I don't remember ever yelling or fighting with my dad and Jeannette; I was just so happy to be there with them where things were stable and peaceful. The one thing I constantly got in trouble for was not doing my homework. Teachers would always say they loved having me in class, but I didn't turn in any work. It was a given that I would always get in trouble during the week of parent-teacher conferences.

When I was with my dad and Jeannette, I got to be a kid, and that was really important to me since I wasn't really able to function as a child when I was with my mom. There was a lot of back and forth, and I was with them only half of the time until I was a senior in high school. I know they let it be my choice, but I do wish they would have had me stay with them full-time sooner.

My dad had been married to my mom, and he knew who she was and what she was capable of. I feel like I spent time with my mom purely out of obligation, and she often manipulated me; going back and forth wasn't great for my mental health. I understand why my parents wanted to allow me to make my own decisions about spending time with her, but I think having the decision made for me would have helped me avoid the pressure and strain of her manipulation.

My parents did several things well to blend us as a family. They never had separate events for us. We did things together as a family, and that was just how it was from the start. Even when Danie and I weren't talking, I would go to her games. There were also special one-on-one events with each parent, but it was rarely my dad with my sister and me, and Jeannette with her biological children going off and doing separate things together. I think that helped so much with our relationship development. We acted as one family, and there was never a chance for us to perceive our situation as two separate families living in the same house.

They handled the situation with Danie and me as well as they could have. They didn't harass us to connect or try to force us to talk. They did sometimes make jokes about our attitudes when the four of us were together. They would make comments like, "Are you guys okay sitting that close to each other?" Despite their attempts at comic relief, our parents were patient and understanding. They operated with the wisdom that any kind of genuine bond or connection between us had to come in its own time and could not be forced. Danie and I didn't fight; we just didn't acknowledge each other's presence, and as difficult as that may have been for our parents to witness, they rarely intervened.

> Another thing my dad and Jeannette have always been masterful at is providing unwavering support for each of us.

Another thing my dad and Jeannette have always been masterful at is providing unwavering support for each of us. There are so many memories and variations of this, but a few that really stand out. I lived in Seattle for six years, and they would do random things to make sure I felt loved and supported. For example, one time they flew out there to support me in a twenty-minute performance at an adult improvisation show. When my sister moved into a new house in Alaska and needed help getting settled, Jeannette flew out there and stayed for a week to help her. We've all needed different types of support at different times, and I truly believe they've both done whatever they could to provide it. It may look different depending on our specific needs, but that's okay because we all know we have that unconditional love and support.

My dad, no matter what he was going through at the time, has always been the king of unconditional support. I recall being fifteen and telling him two weeks before school started that I wanted to join a sport. I had never touched a ball in my life. He didn't even blink. He was like, "Okay, let's go to the store." We went and bought everything I could possibly need for any potential fall sport. If I told my dad I was interested in something, he would be like, "Okay, let's do it. If it is what you want, we'll do it, and we'll do it the best that we can."

He and Jeannette had a rule for our family that if we joined a sport (or really anything) there was no quitting for at least the first season or year. I needed that rule because the first week of volleyball was hell week. I ended up puking in front of the entire team on my first day. Jeannette and my dad remained unified on the quitting rule, but I always knew I had at least two steadfast fans. Despite hectic schedules and loads of responsibilities, they always supported all of us as much as they possibly could. I know we've all felt that in various ways throughout our lives; it would be impossible not to. They showed us what true dedication to family and unconditional love looks like.

It takes a lot of intentionality to blend families.

There are a few pieces of advice I can share based on my experiences. It takes a lot of intentionality to blend families. Teenagers and preteens already don't like being told what to do, let alone by someone they feel like they don't know very well. Patience and authenticity are key. I also think portraying a united front is extremely important. When one of my parents decided on something, the other would agree with them, at least in front of us. Who knows if there were disagreements behind closed doors? If so, we never saw it. As I already mentioned, acting as a family unit as much as possible is critical. It is detrimental to separate the family members to do what is comfortable. I've learned that the more you are forced to sit in uncomfortable moments, the less often they will be uncomfortable and the more growth you will experience.

Finally, therapy is invaluable. It is imperative, though, to find the right therapist. I had a few false starts with therapists that proved to be more harmful than helpful. I started therapy at the age of seven. I went to a play therapist. She had toys and games in her office. She would play games with me and get me to talk about things. Then, she always told my dad what we talked about, and I hated that. It completely destroyed my trust. I think therapy needs to be confidential unless there is a mandatory reporting issue, no matter the age of the child.

Even as an adult, I've had good therapists and therapists that did not help me at all. I had one a year and a half ago that was completely ineffective. I always felt angry when I left. We never accomplished anything. I'd try to go deep, and she would bring me back up to the surface. She acted as a life vest preventing me from going deeper when that was exactly what I needed to do. I was like, "I don't want to talk about my day. I can do that with my friends." She didn't get it, so she had to go. Thankfully, I have also had great therapists, and I still find therapy to be invaluable. It has helped me grow as an individual and become more comfortable with who I am and accepting of what I've been through.

The blending of our families has been a bit rocky at times, but overall smooth. Our parents have modeled resilience, patience, and a fierce devotion to family. We have each been allowed to embrace our individualism while also having our sense of belonging nurtured. Ultimately, this has helped me understand and appreciate the unique spice and flavors that each of us contributes to our family.

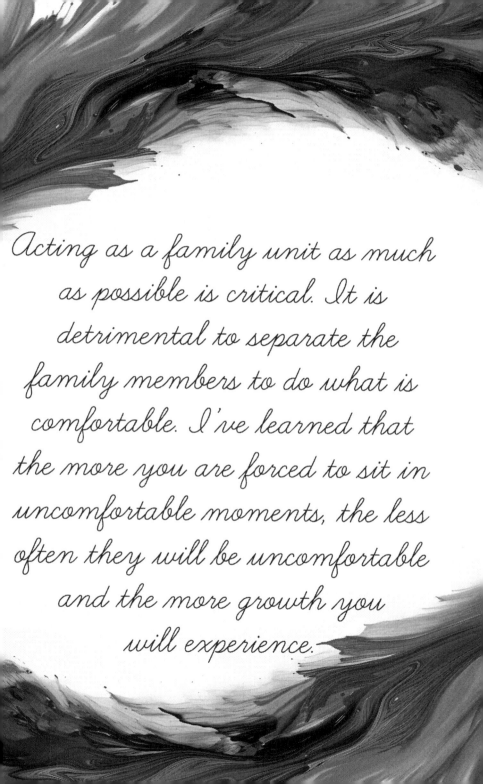

Acting as a family unit as much as possible is critical. It is detrimental to separate the family members to do what is comfortable. I've learned that the more you are forced to sit in uncomfortable moments, the less often they will be uncomfortable and the more growth you will experience.

Danie

It's intriguing to think about what a child's mind chooses to store in long-term memory. I was nine years old when my parents divorced; I don't remember much from that time. Even though they had separated first, I recall being shocked when they followed through with the divorce.

There was only one fight between my parents that I remember, and I'm guessing I only remember that one because my dad fell, and it was funny. I'm grateful for my limited memories of the turmoil that I now know was swirling behind the scenes. I have many friends and acquaintances who have had to live through nasty parental separations and divorces. My parents handled their divorce in a way that was as healthy and positive as it possibly could have been, and I respect them so much for that.

So, what *do* I remember? I remember that once they were separated, it was hard to go to my dad's and leave my mom alone. I had a good relationship with my dad, but I've always been closest to my mom. I was possessive and protective of her. I also felt protective of my relationship with my dad. Looking back, I guess I was also protective of the remaining relationship my parents had, even though they were no longer together. I had no illusion that they would ever get back together, but I still wanted to help preserve what remained between them.

I remember silly things, like when my mom got a new phone and told me that her boss bought it for her. Later, I found out that she had gotten it from Paul. I now understand that she was trying to protect us; she didn't want to introduce him into our lives before she knew he was worthy.

I vividly recall the day that she finally did tell us about him. I had just gotten out of the shower. She held out a picture of a tall man proudly holding a fish he had caught as she explained that she was dating him and wanted us to meet him. I'm sure I cried; it would have been easier than expressing the anger that I remember feeling. Paul was introduced to us before my dad had started to date other people. This was the first time I was confronted with the possibility of my parents dating other people, and I was not interested in sharing my mother with anyone or having someone try to replace my dad.

Soon after being presented with the fish picture and the prospect of meeting Paul came the day we were to meet. A local bowling alley had been chosen as a fun and non-threatening place to bring our two families together. I recall rushing out the door with my mom and brothers to meet Paul and, as it turned out, his daughters.

I wore a yellow shirt and purple sweats because the clothes I had planned to wear were dirty. In fact, what I distinctly remember most about the now infamous bowling date is what I was wearing, what Mariah was wearing, and Paul's hands on my mother's back. I was embarrassed about my outfit to begin with, but even more so when I saw Mariah. She was wearing a pink Cami and a white jean jacket; she looked adorable. And to make matters worse, she was friendly and open to chatting with us. As she tried to make welcoming small talk, I was internally screaming, *DO NOT* talk to me! I remember watching Paul with his hands on my mom's back and wanting to rip him to shreds. And I remember that we went to our house afterward for smothered burritos. The clothing, the food, and the big stranger with his hand on my mother's back. These are the things that I remember most about that first meeting.

Looking back, I can find humor in my memories, even though the events themselves were confusing and painful at the time. I don't think there is anything my mother and Paul could have done differently or better for our introductory meeting. I was who I was—a ten-year-old girl with a strong personality, and I was going to be a brat no matter what.

Later during their courtship, I found a flip-flop-shaped keychain Paul had brought my mother after he'd been on some business trip. The words "I Love Paul" emblazoned on its surface infuriated me. Whenever they weren't around, I'd find it and gnaw on it with a vengeance. My intentions were one hundred percent malicious. I wanted to rip it apart the way I'd wanted to rip Paul apart at that first meeting. I confessed my keychain crimes much later. And still many years after that, Paul presented me with an "I love Paul" keychain during his speech on my wedding day. By then, he did, in fact, have my hard-won love. We still laugh about it all to this day.

As we all spent more and more time together, Paul was careful and wise in his approach with me. He held me at a distance rather than trying to force me to talk to him or like him. I was, in fact, fiercely determined not to like him or get to know him, not because of who he was as a person, but because of the nature of the entire situation. It was a lot to process for a ten-year-old; this is much more obvious as an adult looking back.

To his credit, Paul never tried too hard and truly gave me the space and time that I needed.

To his credit, Paul never tried too hard and truly gave me the space and time that I needed. He was extremely patient for many years, allowing me to gradually warm up to him in my own time. If he hadn't been that way, the relationship may very well have remained cold and distant rather than blossoming into what it is today.

From the beginning, Mariah and Ashley were fine with their dad being with my mom and open to getting to know us. It seemed like they were craving a strong female presence, and they were finding that in my mom. My brothers and I just happened to be part of the package deal they were getting. We didn't talk about their mom, so I knew little of what they had been through with her. My approach was to keep my guard up and steer clear of them whenever I could. Because Mariah and I were only about a year apart, I probably paid the most attention to her. I saw her as my direct competition, and I despised her almost as much as I despised Paul. I remember being constantly annoyed by everything she did. I was young and dramatic and often disgusted by her mere presence.

After that first meeting at the bowling alley, things moved quite quickly. I think my mom and Paul were married by the time I was eleven. The time between bowling and the engagement is a blur for me. I remember a barrage of intense feelings, but not many specific events or situations. Mostly, I was a walking bundle of adolescent frustration, confusion, and anger.

I do remember lying in bed one night with my door open just a crack and listening in horror as my mother told whoever she was talking to on the phone that she was engaged. The tears came fast and furious at first, then faded to a slow, salty drizzle as I cried myself to sleep, frustrated and frightened by all of the uncontrollable changes in my life.

In thinking about the weeks leading up to the wedding, images emerge of the house we grew up in. I watch it fade into the background as we drive away from it and towards the new house we are all about to inhabit and our new lives as one family. We made several trips between the two houses, and the new one felt so far away from my old home and my old life. It felt pretty devastating to the eleven-year-old version of me.

As we struggled to settle into life as a blended family after the wedding, I remained cautious and distant. I was still in no hurry to develop a relationship with Paul or his daughters, even though we were living under the same roof. My mom and Paul were cautious as well. If they had attempted to force relationships between all of us, the results would have most definitely been toxic.

Mariah and Ashley had complicated relationships with their mother, and I vaguely understood that. She would invade our daily lives in weird ways from time to time. Once, when I was in sixth grade and home alone, she threatened to come to our house. My best friend's dad had to come and get me because there was concern that she would actually show up, and nobody knew exactly what she was capable of. I didn't know a lot about her, but there were things that Paul and my mom shared with all of us out of concern for our safety and well-being. At my young age, it never really occurred to me what that must have been like for my new stepsiblings.

Ashley, Mariah, and I seemed to have so little in common. I was a girly girl and very much a mama's girl, unlike them. I couldn't put my finger on it then, but it was clear that our early life experiences were very different. Our interests were very different too.

I didn't think about or care about Ashley since she was much older than I was. Our relationship developed later when I went to college. I had to think about Mariah, though. She lived in the same house as I did, *and* we went to the same high school. That was tough. I really did not like her; she was a new and ever-present annoyance in my life. There was this unspoken competition between us (at least in my mind), and I was determined to win.

As I worked to navigate my early high school years and the attempts to blend our families at home, I held tight to my relationship with my mom. I felt and saw her building relationships with Ashley and Mariah, but that rarely bothered me because she did a fantastic job of always making me feel special. I don't remember any intense feelings of jealousy. I did experience some slight annoyance when I learned about a visit my mom had taken to the mountains with Mariah, Paul, and Ashley early on in the relationship. That annoyance most likely sprung from a sort of surprised confusion that she would have ever gone and done that without me and my brothers.

Holidays were also challenging. My brothers and I would spend Christmas Eve with one parent, and Christmas Day with the other. When Mariah stopped seeing her mom, it bothered me that she would get the whole Christmas with my mom and Paul, and we'd have to go with my dad. I love my dad and had no issues with spending time with him, but I was extremely protective of that time and relationship with my mom.

As I matured, my relationships with my new family members gradually did too. When Mariah and I were the only two kids living at home, and I became more involved and secure at school, things gradually improved between us. This really wasn't until my senior year and beyond, though. It probably took me just as long to learn to trust and accept Paul.

After I graduated from high school, my dad moved to Wyoming. At the time, the move didn't have a huge impact on me. I'd been spending more time with my mom anyway and was about to go off to college. We had a strong relationship, and I wasn't worried about the move damaging that. My dad always did as well as he could with my mom's relationship with Paul. He never spoke poorly about Paul, and my mom and Paul never spoke poorly of him. I don't think he ever really encouraged my having a relationship with Paul; we just didn't talk about it. I'm guessing this did add to my hesitancy with Paul at first, at least subconsciously.

> " He'd probably told me that hundreds of times before but had never gotten a response from me. I sometimes wonder if he remembers that moment the way I do. "

I grew up a lot in late high school. By the time I was ready for college, I felt I knew and could trust Paul. He and my mom moved me to college in southern California, which felt like a million miles from home. It was in that extremely emotional moment that they were getting ready to leave that I told Paul I loved him for the first time. It had been almost eight years since he'd come into my life. What can I say? I'm stubborn! He hugged me and told me he loved me, and I said it back. He'd probably told me that hundreds of times before but had never gotten a response from me. I sometimes wonder if he remembers that moment the way I do.

I remember a noble but failed attempt at getting me support through therapy when I was around eleven. I was not in a place to share my experiences or feelings, and I had little control over my emotions. I was having a difficult time dealing with the trauma I had experienced and was still experiencing as a result of my parents' divorce, so I cried a lot. I had such strong negative feelings about everything Paul, Mariah, Ashley, and divorce, and I wasn't willing or able to express them effectively at that time, especially to a stranger. I only agreed to spend time with a therapist once or twice and shared very little about how I was truly feeling. I chose instead to share what I could manage to express with my mom. I'm not sure how or why the therapy attempts ended, but I think if my parents had encouraged me to try it again when I was a bit older, it could have been beneficial.

Family vacations did help us bond, especially Mariah and me. We found ourselves immersed in non-threatening environments that allowed us to relax and let our guards down a bit, so we could begin to truly get to know each other. I specifically recall our trips to Mexico, when we would stay at the orphanage and play soccer together with the kids there. We ended one of the trips in a bougie hotel in Cancun, so we got to experience and learn from those very different extremes together. Those trips also strengthened my relationship with Paul and showed me how much he truly cared about me. I wasn't his kid, but he was willing to take me places and show me amazing new things. This meant a lot to me and strengthened my emerging feelings of safety and trust.

As previously mentioned, I think Paul was extremely cautious, patient, and strategic with me. I was in competitive softball in high school, and my dad coached me. Paul did a great job of letting that be my thing with my dad. He never tried to force himself into that situation or sports with me, or even give me advice. I know that being more involved with that is something he probably would have enjoyed doing, but he considered me and my relationship with my dad first. Looking back, I really appreciate the selfless approach he took with that.

My mom did a great job of nurturing our special bond while also working to build connections with Mariah and Ashley. I had been the only girl in my family for a long time and had been so close to my mom my entire life. With the addition of Ashley and Mariah came unspoken competition and insecurity. My mother did a wonderful job of building relationships with them and simultaneously always making me feel special. That's been extremely important to me, even as I've grown older. She's gained two daughters, but I don't have to compete with them. I've never had to doubt that I am and will always be her girl.

My mom and Paul were very careful about offering guidance to and disciplining their own children, especially in the beginning of the relationship. I think this was wise at the time. If you are going to blend families, it is crucial to know your kids well. If Paul had tried to come in and parent me right away, things really would have spiraled, and I'm not sure where we'd be today. I listened and responded to my mom more than I would have ever responded to him, and they both knew and respected that.

Now that I am older, and they have been together for so long, their rule about only disciplining or advising their own biological children drives me crazy at times. We are truly a blended family and have been for quite a while. Sometimes, I think it would be appropriate for them to step in more when one of my siblings might need guidance or redirection. My mother and Paul each communicate in such different ways. Neither is right or wrong, necessarily, but those different styles tend to work better in different situations. My mom will ask questions and make you really think about things. Paul is more like, "This is the way it is," and he naturally doesn't always understand or entirely see the female perspective. There have been times that I felt my mom could have stepped in a bit more with Ashley and Mariah. Her approach may have been more effective and made a positive difference. Again, Paul is not a bad communicator, it's just that sometimes she sees things he doesn't and vice versa.

There have also been times when I felt Paul could have been more of a male presence with my brothers as well. He did step in when it was truly needed, but I think he has held back more than necessary. After we had all settled in as a blended family, I just felt at times that they focused too intently on only parenting their biological children. That's just my humble opinion, and truth be told, I like that they do that with me! Even to this day, it probably wouldn't go well if Paul tried to redirect me. He hasn't needed to, though, because my mom is and has always been brutally honest with me.

I do love and respect Paul and want to know what he has to say about things. Especially now that I am older, I truly value his insights and opinions. My husband and I often rely on him for his wisdom and advice, and I'm so grateful that we can.

At the end of the day, I feel blessed that my mom, dad, and Paul handled something so truly traumatic in my young life with patience, positivity, and grace. Of course, mistakes were made along the way, but overall, the divorce and subsequent blending of our families were in healthy and selfless ways. I respect all three of them so much for that. I am lucky to now have three parents and great relationships with each of them. I can be completely honest with them and feel that they all respect me and what I have to say. I've always been a mama's girl, and as I've grown older, I realize more and more that I'm exactly like my mom. We might not look alike, but we are the same in every other way. That is something that I'm proud of, and I'm thankful that she was able to find true happiness and, in the process, incorporate three amazing people into our family. There have, of course, been growing pains along the way, but ultimately, I have grown to love each of them deeply.

Today, when people ask how many siblings I have, I tell them I have two brothers and two sisters. There is a difference in the relationships between my brothers and me and my relationships with Ashley and Mariah. I have always seen my brothers as my protectors, and I go to them first if there is something I need. Ashley, Mariah, and I still have very different personalities, and still don't have a lot in common. However, I do think we've all grown to understand and appreciate each other. Ashley and Christian both have children, and I love being an aunt. It's a bit more challenging to develop close relationships with Ashley's kids because they live in Alaska, but I do adore all of my nieces and nephews!

I can confidently say that we are truly a blended family. Are we always the perfect medley? No. We still struggle with differences and conflict just as any family would. We've all forged unique relationships, and like any relationship, they are each a work in progress with their own highs and lows. What I've learned over the years is that the hard conversations and work necessary to strengthen and maintain each relationship are well worth the effort. It may have taken me several years of simmering to get here, but I wouldn't trade my blended family for anything.

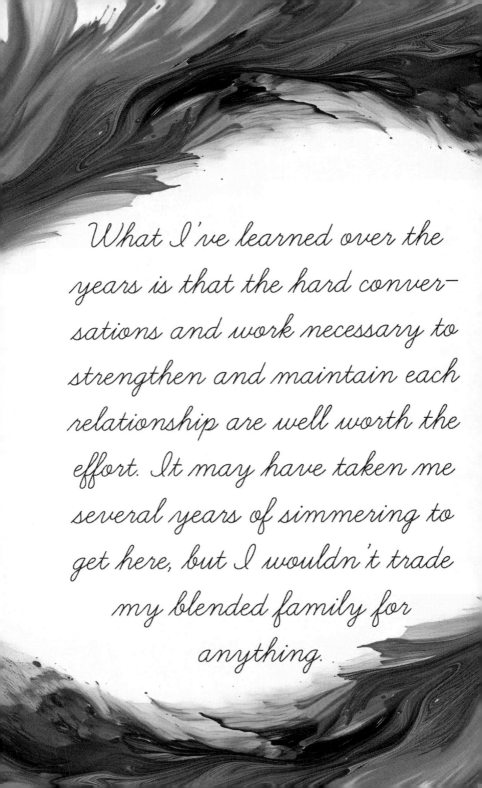

What I've learned over the years is that the hard conversations and work necessary to strengthen and maintain each relationship are well worth the effort. It may have taken me several years of simmering to get here, but I wouldn't trade my blended family for anything.

Part Five

Perfecting the Blend

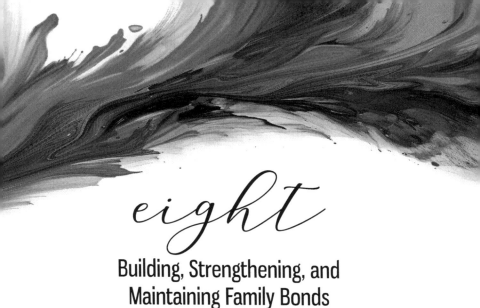

eight

Building, Strengthening, and Maintaining Family Bonds

"A family doesn't need to be perfect, it just needs to be united."
Anonymous

Intentionality is a critical ingredient for taking your blended family to the next level, especially after the kids leave the nest and begin functioning as adults. When everybody was still living at home, we would have dinner together most nights. Throughout my first marriage, we always had dinner together as a family. When Paul and I got together, that was something that he and the girls joined us for right away. It was a great way to ensure at least some time every day where we could sit together and connect, even as our individual lives grew more hectic and took us in different directions. We've committed to continuing that routine with our adult kids as frequently as possible.

We do family dinners at least once a month. Gathering around the table together has forged stronger links between all of us. We've always done birthdays together as a family from the very beginning, and in our family, there is pretty much a birthday every month. Sometimes, we have dinner and game nights. We love to play *Catch Phrase* as a family. It's a great way to not only stay connected as a family but also continue to build memories together.

As highlighted earlier, vacationing together helped us sustain and strengthen our relationships. This is a tradition we've also continued to embrace with our adult children. We each have our own mental collage of beautiful memories from our travels together. One snapshot captures the time we took the kids deep sea fishing. It was their first time, and every time a line went into the water, someone was pulling in a fish. This memory is filled with laughter and beaming smiles and leads to another. Since Anthony is a chef, he cooked up the day's catch for us that night for dinner. He prepared all this fish in four different, delectable ways. It was amazing!

There have also been family cruises. It took some time, but we all finally talked Paul into trying a cruise. We all went to California a few days early and visited Sony Studios. Anthony was in the Marine Corps then, so couldn't go on the cruise, but he met us in California a few days before the cruise and went to Sony with us. I'm so grateful that he's part of these particular memories. That first cruise was amazing, and now we are hooked.

We love doing the cruises together because everybody has their own space and can choose their activities and adventures during the day. Then we always meet up for dinner and spend time together in the evenings. Dinners on the cruises have always been the best. There have been occasions when we've lingered until late into the night, engaging in lively conversations, sharing laughter, and relishing each other's company to the point where the staff had to kick us out.

On one special family cruise, Christian proposed to Heather. He made arrangements with the maître de of the restaurant to present a plate with the words, *Will you marry me?* spelled out on it. The funny thing was that they spelled *marry* as *merry*. So, we have this picture of the ring sitting on that plate from when the waiter brought it over and presented it to Heather. The next morning, I (Paul) remember Heather and I chatting in the gift shop. I remember the look on her face the moment that I revealed we'd be paying for her cruise. She gave me a huge hug and told us how excited she was to be joining our family. The memory warms my heart and reminds me that another perk of being a blended family is the way that it continues to grow.

A quick mental scan for another memory reveals an image of an animated Paul negotiating with some men outside of a gate in Mexico. We had learned that excursions would cost us between sixty and seventy dollars per person. His negotiating skills scored us an old rental bus and some local, unofficial tour guides for just $400 for the day. Heather, Christian's wife, was convinced we were all going to be murdered. It turned out to be an amazing day. They took us to a secluded resort with a private beach. Heather was pleasantly surprised and relieved. She wondered out loud if Paul had some sort of magical insight when, really, he'd just turned out to be very lucky. We've loved every adventure that we've been blessed to enjoy together and are excited to add many more images to our mental collages.

We know we've been blessed to have the time and resources to vacation together as a family. We're also very aware that we cannot become complacent about continuing to preserve and build upon our relationships with each of our kids as they get older and busier. It's necessary to be even more intentional once they are adults themselves. They get busy with their own lives, and they will always automatically have some sort of relationship with their biological parents. With the stepparent, however, it is just different; it takes continuous effort. I (Jeannette) talk to Mariah often because she lives close to us; however, Ashley lives in Alaska, and I am not always great at reaching out to her. We *Facetime* her to see the grandkids, but I don't reach out to just her as much as I'd like to. That's something I feel I could keep working on. Paul spends time with Danie because he sees her regularly. With the boys, it's different and a bit more sporadic. You have to be intentional. If you aren't, it just doesn't happen.

I (Paul) have an acquaintance who has step kids that are in their twenties. His oldest stepdaughter is twenty-eight. He mentioned at one point that he hadn't talked to her for at least six months. He lives in Wisconsin, and she lives in Georgia. So, they *Facetime* on the holidays, but he isn't reaching out to her otherwise. He shared that the relationship just isn't the same as it used to be. This is clearly because he's allowed that distance to grow in the relationship by failing to make an effort to consistently reach out. In pondering my own situation, I am currently very intentional about scheduling one-on-one time with Mariah but need to keep working on it with the others. Jeannette is great about spending quality one-on-one time with each of the kids who live near us, and it is reflected in the quality of their relationships.

As kids get older and build their own lives, they are unlikely to reach out to you just for the sake of staying connected. You must make the effort and avoid using busyness as an excuse. Chances are, you aren't too busy for your own kids or to do the things you love to do, so be intentional about maintaining and continuing to nourish the relationships with your stepchildren. Nurturing those relationships is really making a short and long-term investment.

We have also reflected upon and discussed what the relationships will look like if and when one of us passes away. If you don't have intentional relationships with your step kids, what happens when their biological parents are gone? Will they maintain the relationship with you? Will your biological children maintain the relationship with your significant other when you are gone? It's really important to think not only about the here and now but also what things will look like in the future. The individual relationships within a family are like bridges; we want all of our bridges to be strong so that our family remains close throughout all our lives.

Our family is literally always growing. We have five amazing grandkids, and we feel so blessed to share in that awesome experience, even though we may not be biologically connected to them. A great thing about being a stepfamily is that when you have grandkids, they don't know of a time when you all weren't together. They don't know of any difference, and it will be many years before they figure it out, if ever. Jeannette loves the opportunity to be Nana. Some of the grandkids have only one Nana, and some have several. It doesn't matter to them; they know they are extremely loved. We've been in all of their lives since they were born, and it's been an incredible blessing.

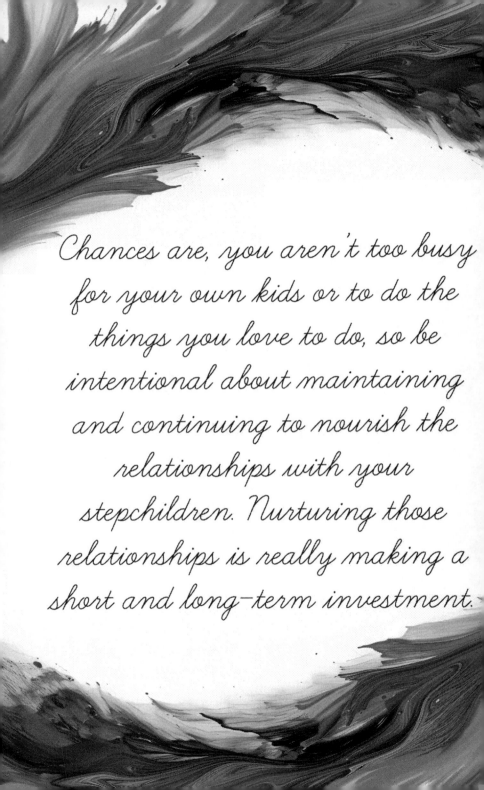

Chances are, you aren't too busy for your own kids or to do the things you love to do, so be intentional about maintaining and continuing to nourish the relationships with your stepchildren. Nurturing those relationships is really making a short and long-term investment.

nine

Older Does Not Equal Easier

Statistics tell us that a growing number of people are divorcing later in life. In fact, according to a study entitled "The Gray Divorce Revolution," by Sandara Brown and I-Fen Lin cited on Lifeway.com, around one in four divorces in this country occur among those who are fifty or older. Because parents are divorcing later in life, many of their children are older, ranging in age from their late teens to their early thirties. We've also learned that there is a strong likelihood that those who divorce in their fifties will get remarried. A logical conclusion is that there are many parents and adult children attempting to make sense of shifting family dynamics and all their places within those shifts. Blending families with older children can bring unique challenges.

We have talked to many people who have attempted and failed to blend their families with adult children. From hairdressers to strangers in airports, to lifelong friends and colleagues, we've heard numerous horror stories about difficulties building and/or maintaining relationships with adult kids. Some families have adult children who refuse to speak to each other. They hold isolated gatherings for the different strands of their families, maintaining those separate family identities. Other couples have been torn completely apart because their adult children didn't adjust to their remarriage or accept the new stepparent. Still others have had older children and/or stepchildren turn biological parents and stepparents against each other, resulting in continuous drama. When emotions are high, negative messages and actions tend to escalate, and situations can deteriorate quickly.

> " *We found open and honest communication and a steadfast commitment to not only each other, but our blended family to be key when navigating this situation.* "

We also know that even when they are establishing their own lives, our kids need us, and sometimes they come back home. We had kids in and out of our house into their late twenties. Regardless of their ages, they still needed us and that stable home environment at various times in their young adult lives for various reasons. Although we were able to navigate this as a couple, we've heard stories about second marriages ending for this very reason. An adult child wants to move back home, and the biological parent supports it, but the stepparent doesn't, causing tension between the couple. If an authentic relationship never had a chance to form between the stepparent and stepchild, it can understandably be more difficult for the parents to be on the same page. Differing parenting styles carried over from previous marriages and family situations can also play a role. We found open and honest communication and a steadfast commitment to not only each other, but our blended family to be key when navigating this situation.

We believe these things often happen because of those false assumptions that once our kids are adults, they don't need the same support that younger children might need when it comes to blending families. Because they are older, the tendency is to assume that they are fine, and that less effort is required to support them in adjusting and blending. The truth is age does not ensure emotional stability or maturity. Divorce, as well as the events leading up to it, can be just as traumatic for a thirty-year-old child as for a thirteen-year-old child.

> **"**
>
> *The impact divorce has on the relationships between children and their biological parents can be detrimental, especially if the proper support isn't provided*
>
> **"**

The impact divorce has on the relationships between children and their biological parents can be detrimental, especially if the proper support isn't provided. The aftermath for adult children, though sometimes not as visible, is real. There are bound to be feelings of grief and loss that need to be acknowledged and dealt with. Older children sometimes end up questioning the possibility of being in long-term relationships themselves as well. If an adult child doesn't work through those emotions, when a parent begins a new relationship, they simmer beneath the surface, often tainting the ability to positively form those new relationships. The importance of consistent and honest communication with older children about how they are truly feeling and what they need cannot be overstated. Without it, existing relationships become distant, and/or the new relationships so important to the blended family dynamic fail to take root.

When blending families, there are two likely scenarios. Either the couple marries, and the children grow up together for at least part of the time, or the couple marries after the kids are out on their own. In the first scenario, it seems fairly obvious that, as parents, we can model what a strong and loving relationship looks like and how to nurture relationships. Looking back, it almost seems like a luxury to have that time to model this and create family habits and traditions while the kids are growing up together. As we've shared, this can and should be continued even after the kids have left the home through family dinners, gatherings, celebrations, and travel.

The second scenario is a bit trickier. Kids that have not grown up together sometimes find themselves thrown into familial relationships they are just expected to accept and be happy about, regardless of differences in personalities, experiences, and often, that lingering trauma from divorce. Assumptions are made that

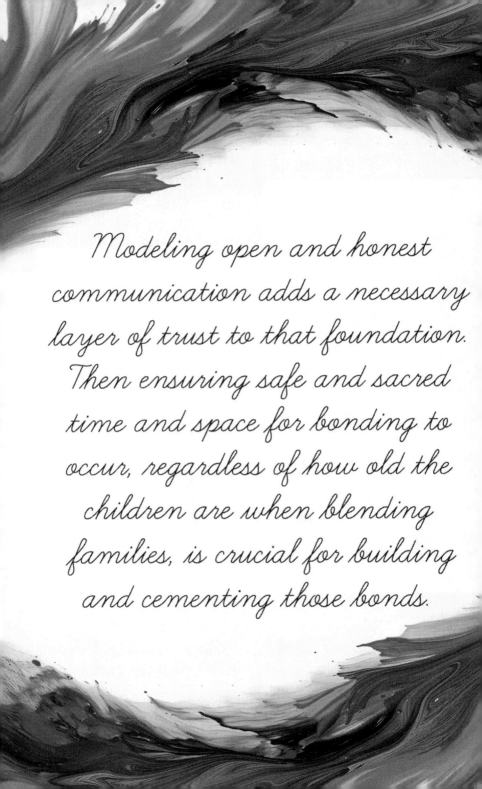

Modeling open and honest communication adds a necessary layer of trust to that foundation. Then ensuring safe and sacred time and space for bonding to occur, regardless of how old the children are when blending families, is crucial for building and cementing those bonds.

they should automatically want to get to know and love strangers-turned-stepsiblings. This is why it is even more crucial to be intentional about laying a strong foundation where everyone involved can have the time and space to grow into the relationships. Modeling open and honest communication adds a necessary layer of trust to that foundation. Then ensuring safe and sacred time and space for bonding to occur, regardless of how old the children are when blending families, is crucial for building and cementing those bonds.

As great as this all sounds, it can be more challenging when the "children" involved are already adults with their own busy lives. It can be more difficult to carve out that time, and the impetus to make it happen consistently and at times that work well will likely fall on you. Another obstacle is that when you bring adult children from your families together, it can be awkward at first, especially if personalities and values differ greatly. Don't let those awkward moments deter you. When relationships are allowed to naturally develop and grow, all family members learn to value them and the family dynamic blossoms as well. If this doesn't happen, there is no reason for adult children to connect, and you can wind up with one of those previously mentioned horror stories to tell.

One way to combat awkward interactions and help adult children get to know each other is finding ways to bring everyone together that are non-threatening and fun. It is important that these gatherings are not just for holidays or formal celebrations, as these can feel especially heavy and create feelings of unnecessary pressure. Events that allow everyone to have the freedom to be themselves and get to know one another in carefree settings can go a long way in creating those bonds. It can also be helpful to invite non-family members to gatherings, so they don't feel so awkward.

We've talked throughout the book about how much nurturing and intentionality is required to blend families. Just as with any family, there are bound to be bumps in the road with blended families. The difference with blended families is that you must be ultra-intentional about cultivating family dynamics in which everyone in the family, regardless of age, feels included and invaluable and cherishes each relationship. If this doesn't happen, it won't feel necessary to nurture those relationships further into adulthood, and any family bonds that have developed can quickly disintegrate. With intentionality, patience, and a dash of resilience, families with children of any age can be successfully blended.

Have the Hard Conversations

Jeannette

Picture this: you're on the verge of celebrating the completion of your book in which you share your advice about how to blend families when a conflict emerges within your own blended family. What begins as a single thread of misunderstanding between stepsiblings unravels with confusion and painful miscommunication for months until it threatens to transform a slight tear into a gaping hole in the family tapestry you've all worked hard to create. As parents and stepparents, you have a decision to make. Do you intervene when the conflict is between adult children, or wait for it to work itself out?

Recently, Danie and Mariah were involved in a conflict. As Mariah was working through some major life changes, Danie was ready and patiently waiting and praying for similar changes in her life. An attempt to communicate how they were each feeling went wrong, and months of awkward interactions and hurt feelings followed. As their parents, we watched in anguish as the conflict deepened, and we saw their relationship deteriorating. I (Jeannette) agonized over whether to intervene. It was going on for eight months with no end in sight, and I began to recognize the impact it was having on me and our family. I had discussed the situation with Danie, mostly acting as a sounding board. As an outsider, I could understand both sides of the conflict and the feelings the girls were grappling with. I could also feel myself pulling away from Mariah, and that's when I knew I had to intervene and have a conversation with her. I was keenly aware that unresolved conflict would just linger beneath the surface of all our interactions, and in turn, erode our relationship.

When something is bothering me, I typically try to give it time, space, and prayer; but when it just doesn't go away, I know it is something I can't ignore. I sought advice from Ashley and Paul. Both strongly advised me to stay out of it. And truthfully, that's what I wanted to do. I was definitely feeling the flight side of *fight or flight*, but I knew I couldn't do that. Ultimately, I am Mariah's stepmother, and I want and need to be there for her. I love her, and I know she loves me. But I have no false illusion that there is no guarantee that she will always love me. With biological children, there is a sense of that unbreakable connection and unconditional love. Your relationships still require nurturing, but you can do and say some nasty things, and they will always love you; they will always come back. With stepchildren, that connection can and should be built and nurtured, but there are no guarantees.

For the sake of our relationship, I had to share how I was feeling and how the conflict was impacting not only our relationship but also seeping into relationships in our family. I had learned through my experiences and years of therapy that it isn't healthy for me or my relationships to stuff my feelings. As parents, worries about overstepping boundaries often stop us from expressing our true feelings, especially when our babies are navigating adulthood. But if you've built that strong family foundation, and your kids value you and your relationship, they will want to hear what you have to say.

As parents, worries about overstepping boundaries often stop us from expressing our true feelings, especially when our babies are navigating adulthood. But if you've built that strong family foundation, and your kids value you and your relationship, they will want to hear what you have to say.

After I scheduled a time for us to meet, I spent some time mentally rehearsing the conversation. I know the power of words, especially during difficult conversations, and I desperately wanted to get this right rather than cause more damage. In the end, it just took one simple question to open the conversation and our line of communication: "How do you think things are going with the family?" I asked. Tears, an immense sense of relief, and an authentic conversation followed.

As difficult as the conversation and the days and weeks leading up to it were, it caused improvement in all the relationships that the conflict was threatening to damage. It's sometimes hard to navigate that fine line when guiding adult children. Again, you want to allow them to be the adults you've raised and work through things independently but also be there for them and share the knowledge you've gained through your own experiences. Anytime you have the opportunity to spare them some heartache, the instinct is to jump in. At times, your advice and guidance are welcomed, and other times, naturally, it may feel intrusive. I have learned an effective technique from my best friend. She starts a difficult conversation with the question, *Can I share something with you?* I love this question because you are asking for permission to offer guidance. It puts the adult child in the driver's seat and disarms defense mechanisms that could arise. The conversation can then feel less like a know-it-all parent imposing opinions on a child and more like authentic and caring communication.

As you've likely gathered by now, Jeannette and I (Paul) have very different communication and conflict resolution styles. Throughout the growing conflict with the girls, and ultimately when she asked for advice about whether to have the difficult conversation with Mariah, I thought we both should stay out of it. I would have just let it go, assuming it would eventually work out. And that would have been a mistake. I can now clearly see into that alternate future, the one where Jeannette took my bad advice. Mariah and Danie would have likely been cordial to each other at family gatherings, but they would not have been sisters. And they would not have been happy. Jeannette was one hundred percent correct with her approach; she had to be a leader in the situation. That is what we need to do as parents of adult children. Even after our kids have morphed into adults with their own mortgages, jobs, cars, and money, we are still their parents. They will still depend on us for leadership and guidance. It's part of the beauty of being a parent in a blended family, and really any family with adult children. We have the privilege of being friends, confidants, and leaders with and for our adult children.

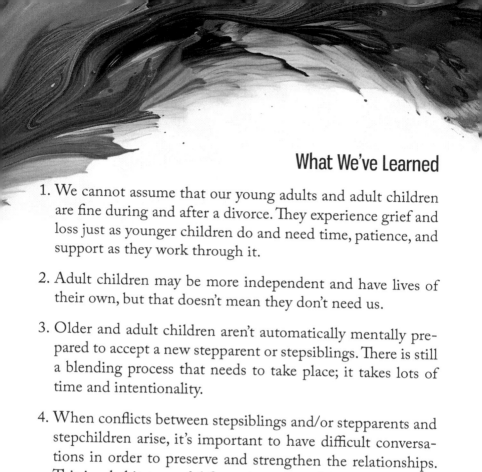

What We've Learned

1. We cannot assume that our young adults and adult children are fine during and after a divorce. They experience grief and loss just as younger children do and need time, patience, and support as they work through it.

2. Adult children may be more independent and have lives of their own, but that doesn't mean they don't need us.

3. Older and adult children aren't automatically mentally prepared to accept a new stepparent or stepsiblings. There is still a blending process that needs to take place; it takes lots of time and intentionality.

4. When conflicts between stepsiblings and/or stepparents and stepchildren arise, it's important to have difficult conversations in order to preserve and strengthen the relationships. This is a habit to model from the onset of the blending process.

ten

Blessings upon Blessings

"Preach the Gospel at all times, and if necessary, use words."
–attributed to Francis of Assisi

A few months before I met Paul, God spoke to me. Around the same time that my ex-husband and I had separated, my brother-in-law and his wife also separated. I was very close to her. We had a small group of friends that would go out to bars. Deep down, I knew I wasn't going to find a partner or start a relationship in a bar. I decided to stop going, then God spoke to me. He said, "Be patient, I have something very special for you." I didn't know what he meant then, but now I know, without a doubt, that it was Paul.

Our biggest goal in writing this book was to help families who may be going through or preparing to go through the blending process. We've reflected upon and learned from many experiences, with our friends, extended families, and five amazing kids. We've done some things well, and there are things we would definitely do differently if we were to do it all again. Throughout it all, our faith has been our guide.

We are Christians and would never deny our faith. We choose to share our story and strive to model our faith. We know, without a doubt, that God brought us together. That's not to say that

God wants people to get divorced. God is sovereign—the Alpha and Omega—beginning and the end. He has orchestrated the whole thing. He knew, well before we did, that we would each get divorced. God has the power to do anything. He could have restored our first marriages.

> When you surrender to God's will, you can see what he has in store for you. We both strive to have our decisions and actions align with our faith.

As humans, he allows us to have free choice and make our own decisions. He uses whatever circumstances come out of our choices to lead us in a certain way. Our humanness caused us to marry our first partners, but we both know that wasn't God's will. Life, as a result, was extremely difficult for both of us for a period of time. However, there were still numerous blessings that came during and within those initial relationships. When you surrender to God's will, you can see what he has in store for you. We both strive to have our decisions and actions align with our faith. Divorce didn't align for either of us, but God used it to bring us together.

We have a strong faith, both individually and as a couple. We pray together every day. We pray for our kids, for what is going on in each other's lives, and for all our loved ones. Praying together has strengthened our relationship. We also attend church together and are connected to a wonderful church community. When you are part of a community like this, you have a strong support system made up of people who can pick you up when you need it. They are there throughout the good and the bad, encouraging and praying for you.

While our church community is invaluable to us, we have not pressured our kids to attend a certain church or practice religion in a certain way. Two of our children attend church, but not to our church, and that is okay. We know that it is their path. For the others, in their own time and in God's time, maybe they will go to church as well. It's very dangerous to force your religion upon your kids (or anyone for that matter). When you do this, it isn't likely to truly become theirs; they are just doing it for you.

For us, our faith is such a part of who we are as individuals and our relationship. It helped create and strengthen our bond from the beginning and has helped guide us through some challenging times. I think about how patient and loving Paul was with Danie. If he hadn't been a believer with strong faith, he may not have been able to handle that difficult situation the way he did for as long as he did.

It is not lost on us that we are extremely blessed. We have a big, beautiful, blended family that continues to bond and grow. Our experiences have shaped who we are to each other and as parents. We hope our marriage is a model to our kids and to others. We don't want to come off as aggressive, religious people because that can just push people further away from religion and God. We aren't quiet about who we are; again, our ultimate goal is to lead and live by example.

Our journey hasn't been perfect, but it has been amazing. As a couple, we continue to strive to embody unconditional love, compassion, and understanding. We want to show everyone in our lives that, although we have our own struggles, we consistently lean on God and each other for support and strength. We believe that the key ingredients of our faith and love have helped guide us in merging our two families into a harmonious whole. We also know that the journey isn't over and that we'll need to continue to learn, grow, and enhance our relationships. Whether you are in the midst of or just embarking upon your journey, we hope you find our story to be part of your recipe for great success.

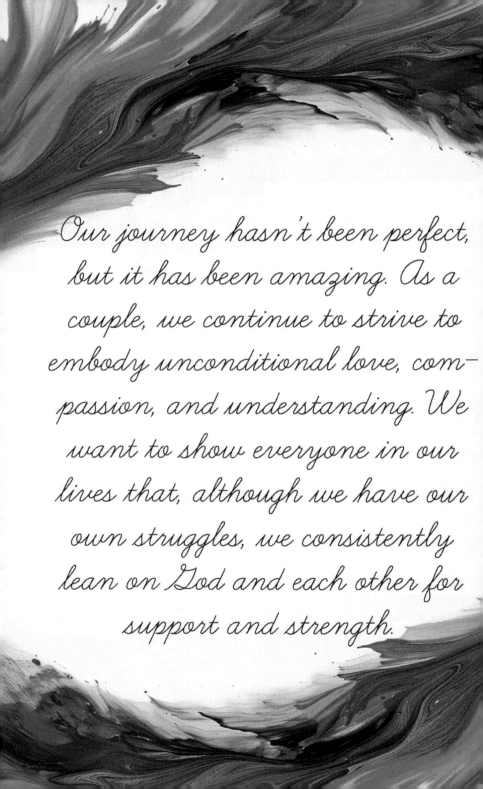

Our journey hasn't been perfect, but it has been amazing. As a couple, we continue to strive to embody unconditional love, compassion, and understanding. We want to show everyone in our lives that, although we have our own struggles, we consistently lean on God and each other for support and strength.

Acknowledgments

We would like to thank Jacalyn Huston for helping us put our thoughts and stories into words. We couldn't have done this book without her. She was able to collect our thoughts and stories and put them on paper, making this book very content-rich.

We would also like to thank each of our children for their honest and transparent input on what it has been like to grow up in our stepfamily. Each of their journeys has been unique, especially when it comes to the time it took for them to feel comfortable with our new family dynamics.

We would also like to thank Janelle Evangelides for being our guide to the world of social media. She has played such an instrumental part in getting our message out to the people who most need to hear it.

We also want to thank God for walking with us and guiding us during our blended family journey. Our faith has played a huge role in our journeys. We've relied on it as we waded through the experiences of healing from childhood trauma and our divorces, beginning our lives together, and merging our families.

About the Authors

Paul and Jeannette Savage have been married for 16 years and have five adult children (Jeannette has 3 kids from her first marriage and Paul has two kids from his first marriage). They also have been blessed with five grandkids. Even with the kids out of the house, they still have an active family life hosting family activities at least every month and caring for grandkids. Jeannette was married for 20 years in her first marriage and Paul was married for 12 years. Paul grew up in Michigan and has lived in Colorado for 36 years. Jeannette was raised in Nebraska and Wyoming and has called Colorado home for 37 years.

Outside of their busy family life, for over ten years Paul and Jeannette have mentored many couples and individuals helping them navigate marital issues before and after their wedding day. Both of them work with people individually providing them the life skills necessary to be successful in life. Jeannette has led women's groups at our church and Paul has led a men's group that has continuously met for 22 years. Paul has also personally coached over 180 men guiding them in recovery from the issues that men struggle with.

Jeannette was in medical field for 20 years and recently retired. Paul has been selling industrial products for 35 years and is currently vice president of sales of a division for a Fortune 500 company. He has traveled extensively all over the world but always loves coming home to his favorite place on the planet: at home with Jeannette and his family in Colorado.

Contact Us

For inquiries regarding speaking engagements and booking information, please feel free to contact us.

📞720-281-7833

✉️JSavage@blendedbook.org

✉️PSavage@blendedbook.org

🌐blendedbook.org

follow us on:

f blendedfamilybook

📷blended_book

t blended_book

Works Cited:

Escape Writers. "Best Short Inspirational Family Quotes." Escape Writers. https://www.escapewriters.com/best-short-inspirational-family-quotes/. Accessed January 7, 2024.

Francis of Assisi. "Quotes by Francis of Assisi." Goodreads. https://www.goodreads.com/author/quotes/149151.Francis_of_Assisi. Accessed November 3, 2023.

Goodreads. "Forgiveness is not an occasional act; it is a constant attitude." Goodreads. https://www.goodreads.com/quotes/57037-forgiveness-is-not-an-occasional-act-it-is-a-constant?scrlybrkr=9925697c. Accessed July 19, 2023.

Goodreads. "The direction you choose to face determines whether you're standing." Goodreads. https://www.goodreads.com/quotes/661320-the-direction-you-choose-to-face-determines-whether-you-re-standing. Accessed February 5, 2024.

Goodreads. "The most important ingredient we put into any relationship is..." Goodreads. https://www.goodreads.com/quotes/7269159-the-most-important-ingredient-we-put-into-any-relationship-is. Accessed February 5, 2024.

Goodreads. "We do not learn from experience. We learn from reflecting." Accessed February 3, 2024. https://www.goodreads.com/quotes/664197-we-do-not-learn-from-experience-we-learn-from-reflecting.

Legit.ng. "43 Trauma Quotes to Help You on Your Journey to Healing." Legit.ng. https://www.legit.ng/ask-legit/quotes-messages/1494938-43-trauma-quotes-journey-healing/. Accessed February 2nd, 2024.

"Lifeway." Reasons People Are Getting Divorced After Fifty, Accessed February 6, 2024, https://www.lifeway.com/en/articles/mature-living-reasons-people-are-getting-divorced-after-fifty.

Smart Stepfamilies. "Marriage & Family: Stepfamily Statistics." Smart Stepfamilies, https://smartstepfamilies.com/smart-help/marriage-family-stepfamily-statistics. Accessed February 5th, 2024.

Youth Dynamics. "It's Survival: 13 Quotes on Trauma Healing." Youth Dynamics, https://www.youthdynamics.org/its-survival-ggggee

Made in the USA
Columbia, SC
06 March 2024

32259646R00104